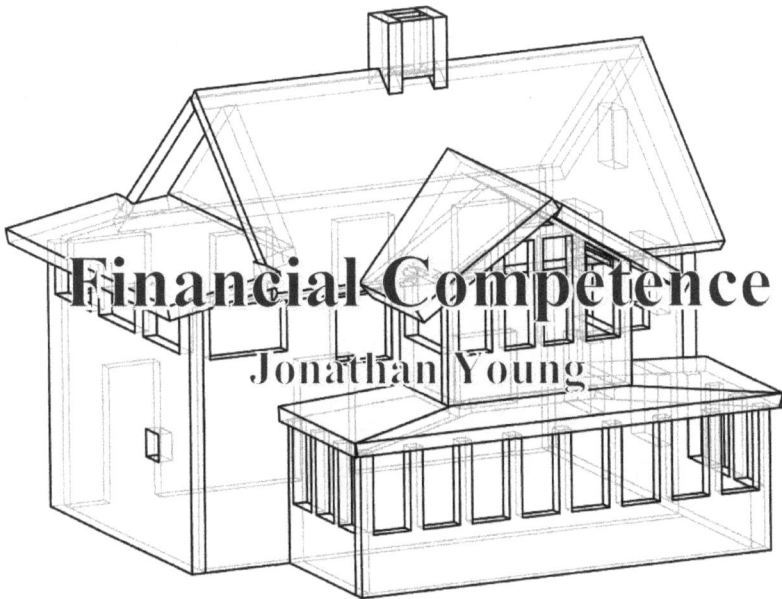

Financial Competence

Jonathan Young

To God, my Father and Lord over my life, for giving me the gifts and ability to share the knowledge that I have.

To my wife, Jasmine, for your love and support during this process-- I thank and love you.

Content

Contents

Introduction

All movement is not progression, though most may view these two concepts synonymously. Constant movement without forethought or retrospection is a losing battle. Yet, most people spend their lives spinning their wheels and never arriving at any destination. Why is this? Is it that the burdens of life are simply too great? Is it that the information to create financial freedom is only available to the elite of society, and the rest of us common people lack will-power? Truthfully, however copious the theories may be, the answer is more obvious than you may think. *It is simply a lack of knowledge, understanding, application, and competence as it pertains to financial basics.*

If given the choice between 10 million dollars and the knowledge of 100,000 books, most would choose the 10 million dollars without a second thought. But according to the Washington Post, about 70% of people who win the lottery or receive a windfall of money go bankrupt within 1-3 years. Now, reading this, you may identify yourself with the other 30%, right? So without suggesting you might be wrong, consider these:

1. Are you in the 78% of Americans that could not cover a $1000 emergency expense without going into debt?

2.   Have you ever gone through a considerable sum of money or a bonus check quickly and had nothing to show for it?

3.   Who would be the top five people you would call first (not necessarily quickly), and do they currently have a 6 or 7-figure net worth now?

4.   Do you track your income and expenses today?

Suppose you answered the first two questions with "Yes" and the last two with "No," unfortunately, you are not in the 30%. If you answered the first two "No" and the last two "Yes," chances are you do not play the lottery at all and are either well on your way to or at lottery ticket earnings now.

This book is not to tear down confidence but to build up competence in finances to begin to take control of your financial life seamlessly. This book is about changing habits and developing understanding while subconsciously building success and financial freedom. The definition of financial freedom as it pertains to this book does not mean flaunting fancy jewelry, cars, houses, or material things. As it pertains to this book, it means being able to take care of household expenses, building net worth to financially pay for your household expenses for a lifetime (Retirement), and having complete control of all aspects of your finances and financial future. This book seeks to uncover strategies that work to make your money work for you instead of you constantly working for money. This is what we know as "retirement," and contrary to popular belief, you do not have to be old in order to be retired. Taking control of your money means directing its path to your freedom.

This illustration on the next page shows two pyramids, the first one, "How You Should Setup Your Finances," is the true financial foundation, and the second, "How Most People Setup Their Finances," is how most people operate their financial lives. This book will go through in detail the foundation method and why it works; it will also show many examples of why the way most people handle their finances don't work. The consequences of not setting up your finances correctly can be dire, and the last thing you will want in life is to wish that you had rather than be glad that you did. On the other hand, the foundation method is the best way to ensure your finances are safe, secure, and growing. Once you have mastered these financial principles, you can overcome almost any obstacle. This mastery is called *Financial Competence*.

1. Financial [fi-nan-shuhl] *noun:* the management, creation, and study of money and investments.
2. Competence ['käm-pə-tən(t)s] *noun:* the quality or state of having sufficient knowledge, judgment, skill, or strength

" ... money can only give happiness where there is nothing else to give it. Beyond a competence, it can afford no real satisfaction ...."
— Jane Austen

The Foundation

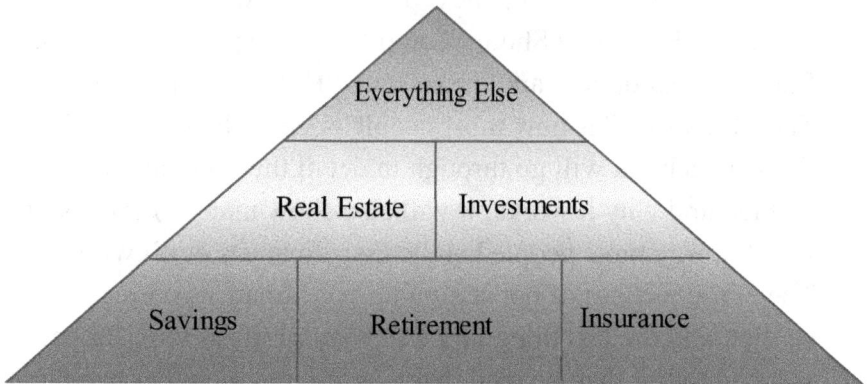

How You Should Setup Your Finance

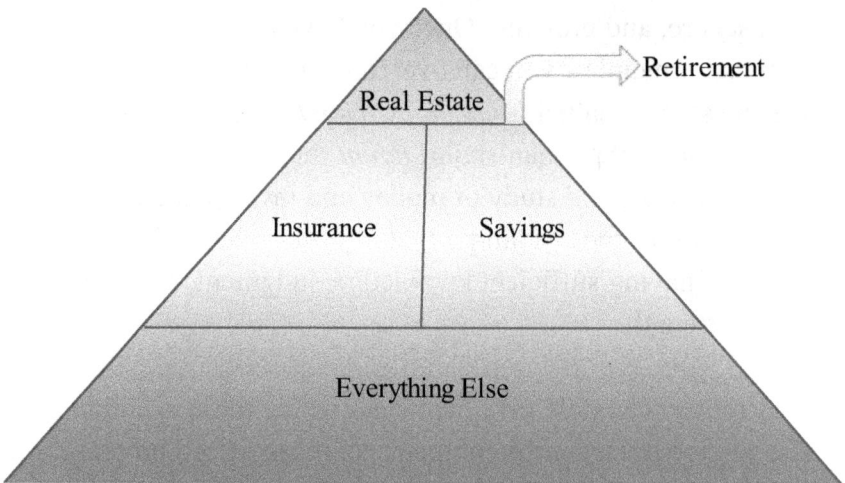

How Most People Setup Their Finances

Financial Life Chart

The Foundation

Savings account & Money marketing account. < **Banker**
Retirement: 401K, Traditional IRA, and Roth IRA. <
**Financial Advisor/ Personal Accountant/ HR
Representative** Life, Health & Property, and Casualty
Insurance. < **Insurance Agent & Attorney**

The Structure

Real estate property ownership.
< **Real Estate Agent/ Loan Officer/ Real Estate Broker.**
Investments: stocks, bonds, mutual funds, ETFs, and 529. <
Investment firm (Organization) Business < **Consultant &
Tax Accountant**

The Ceiling

Everything else < **You have financial competence / make
wise decisions with money** Bills: living expenses, commute
expenses, and Debt payments < **Accountant/ Company
Representatives**

Pouring Cement
Saving, Retirement, & Insurance

A good foundation is the start of a great structure, while a bad or inadequate foundation leads to a path of ruin. The difference between a bad foundation and an inadequate one depends on the size of the building you want to build. If you are a simple person who can happily live on $30,000 per year, then you can create a shallow but sturdy foundation of about $500,000. This may seem like a lot, but it can be done slowly but surely when broken down into small chunks. The first reaction to large numbers in human nature is frustration and even feelings of defeat. How can you save up to six figures when you have never seen more than four figures in your account and for just a brief period? It seems impossible and leaves most feeling like, "If it is out of my reach, why bother?" or "Money isn't everything," followed by, "You only live once; if you save everything and die young, then you would have never lived." Some of these concerns are valid points; however, if you keep living and doing what you have been doing and never see a change in your life, won't you feel tired of all the living and have nothing to show for it? If you are not, keep living and change nothing; if you are, this book is designed for you. This book was written for the simple, the workers that do not make enough for the fancy spreadsheets or the finance jargon mumbo-jumbo; this book was written for those that are not well read and just want a simple path to take control of their finances.

The book is simply about setting up your financial foundation, and with that: What color is your foundation? This may seem like an odd question; the reason is whether you guessed white, grey, or black; the correct answer is who cares if it holds up your home. This is the way your financial foundation is. No one cares about the inner workings of successful people's finances; they just see a person who does not worry about money and can get whatever they want anytime they want it. The stability of the success was based on the depth and breadth of their foundation. This can be deceiving as well, and some get whatever they want, do whatever they want, and do not look as though they are worried about their finances, but they are living life on credit cards, loans, and broken promises. You cannot see their foundation either, and therefore, it can be misleading to know which one to follow. The concept is found in the individual's habits. It will show you how to qualify, which one must have a solid foundation, and which one is on their way to financial despair and ruin. Oh no! Here it comes; this is the part that tells you to sacrifice, suffer, work hard, work smart or cut off all your friends. Right? No!

Just as in a house, building, or structure of any kind, the foundation decides how high and large you can build. This is simply how you set up your success. This part feels the longest, but the results last so much longer. Do not believe it; go online, and look up how old or what year your home, apartment, and any other structure was built. You have heard that the longest part of the building process is the foundation but is that the success of the building? To build the average house, it takes about 1 month to lay down the foundation, about 2 months to frame if the weather allows, and another 4-5 months for the build-out of the home, but the last step most people forget is the lifetime of living in the home. To repeat, "Lifetime of living in the home" means the successful part of building a house is the house does not cave in on you.

Translating this into finances takes a moderately brief period of building your financial foundation, a little bit longer building the structure of your financial future, most of your time building out your finances to the way you want them, and finally, a lifetime of enjoying your financial future. This means that the success of a home is not when it is completed, but the years it goes into being successfully lived in. As for your finances, the same is true. Success is not in the building up of wealth but in the successful lifestyle you get to enjoy for the rest of your lifetime. The foundation is so important because once built, it is virtually indestructible, which is why, when a home is burned down to the ground after a house fire, a new structure can be rebuilt quickly. The same is true as it pertains to your finances; for this reason, when millionaires or even billionaires lose all their money due to some lawsuit, tragedy, or freak accident, once the storm clears, they regain all that they lost. The inverse is also true; could you imagine someone trying to build a ten-story building on the same foundation as a house? Of course not, or if you did, you would expect its collapse. Therefore, the statement about the lottery holds true every time. Those who believe money, or the lack thereof, is the problem are those who have weak or no foundation for their money. Winning the lottery to them is more devastating to them because it is as if a ten-story building is dropped on a home's foundation or no foundation at all. People with nothing or shallow foundations collapse under the pressure causing them to file for bankruptcy, while if you have no foundation, the collapse brings you below the ground. Most are better off having never won the lottery at all. With no further delay, this is day one, building your foundation for the structure you want to live in for the rest of your life.

The Foundation holds the entire Structure
- Find a trustworthy financial institution to place funds into.
- Place funds into checking accounts and assess your monthly earnings.
- Divide said earnings in the following ways:
  - Savings (short-term / long-term)
  - Property/Casualty & Life and Health insurance
  - Set aside for retirement in a money marketing account

Some ways to start this Foundation

1.   As a rule of thumb, always save at least 10% of your monthly income. Then, using a money marketing account, talk with your Banker to learn of ways to invest a small part of your money into mutual funds or bonds. Learn how the market works but avoid getting into something serious without a financial advisor.

2.   Short-term - saving for tier 2 or the structure is the first and most important goal. Meaning you want to save for that down payment on your first property, whether it be a home, condominium, multi-family home, business / commercial property, townhome, or farm. Whether you pay cash or finance, this goal is more important than moving out of home just for the sake of moving out. There are many options out there but do not rent if you do not have to. "Yeah, I think I'm ready to move out. I'm not ready for a home yet, so I think I will rent an apartment until I'm ready to purchase/finance a home." NO, STOP, CTRL+ALT+Delete! The average cost of rent across the country is $1,231, and in Georgia, it is $890 per month (and going up). The average cost of mortgage payment in the United States is $1,061 for a $220,261 home at a 4% interest rate, Google it! With a money marketing account, talk with your Banker to see if there is a way to invest a small part of your money into mutual funds or bonds. Learn how the market works but

do not get into something serious without a financial advisor. Actual amounts: healthy savings look like 6 months to a year worth of monthly income. While young, life, disability, and hospital income policies altogether are about $50 per month. Lastly, regarding retirement accounts, most companies have a retirement program and sometimes offer matching options, which are free money that should always be taken advantage of. Once the account is open, a healthy monthly contribution of 15% of your monthly income should suffice. This puts you in a great predicament for future financial endeavors.

Long-term - this is the 30-year plan for your savings and retirement. Here you plan for the young or non-existent children's college fund, Health Plan, potential disabilities or illnesses, and life insurance. Also, real estate is not just your house, and this is your property portfolio. Tuesday auctions at the courthouse, tax liens, cash purchases, and finance are some of the ways that you can obtain real estate that will ensure your financial success. Once you are situated in your home, look for other much cheaper properties in your area to see if there are any outstanding tax liens unpaid or foreclosure properties that you can either buy outright or finance with a low monthly payment. Fix it up; whether it takes weeks or years, once you finish it, you will have the first investment property that will earn you an average of in Georgia $890, if in the country, $1,231 per month, which could go towards your $1,061 mortgage payments and more. These are, of course, averages, but any income you do not get up every morning for is an income worth having. If you were going to get a second job, get it to build wealth, not for that new car that looks great today, but depreciates tomorrow. Purchase a car that can get you by for now, not something that will keep your debt-to-income ratio High. You want your assets High, not your debt. So, you are thinking, what about credit, low income, a broken system that is not for me? Let us go over a few of the issues I mentioned above.

    o   Credit - on-time payments, credit history, the amount used, accounts opened, and credit available are the main components of your score.

Name one of these factors that do not require you to have assets greater than your debt to reflect well. Do not be so concerned with what someone can loan you today that you forget that you can buy it tomorrow. Credit is your ability to make payments over time. Credit is nowhere in this foundation or structure because it is in the "everything else" category, which is the smallest category in the entire pyramid. Build your foundation (assets), then set up your credit (debt). If you are like most people, you have seen and experienced financial hardships. Well, how many of us have the assets backing us up to keep us afloat during these challenging times? Not many; in fact, 78% of Americans do not even have $1,000 in their account, in savings or otherwise. So, we can conclude we do not save very well or anything on this chart that is in the foundation part. Car loans in America have surpassed mortgages. Credit is a big problem when debt equals too much and assets equal too little. Manage your finances; not the way TV tells you to, "Got debt? Will single-handedly end your chances of financing a home for the next seven years guaranteed, call today!!" is what you should hear every time you hear a commercial that advocates bankruptcy. This is not control; this is relinquishing control by postponing your future of financial competency for the next seven years of your life. The key to credit is never to Finance anything besides property that you do not have the funds available to pay today. What does that mean? Not what they tell you; you can afford only what you see in your account. That new BMW for 50k. Look at your bank account. Do you have 50k + 30k for gas and maintenance as well as six months' worth of savings and/or assets in owned property (not financed) or investment equivalent collateral right now? All jokes aside, this is a real question you should ask yourself before stretching your monthly payments out 10 years to get down to $1,000 per month and still being unable to afford it. It's funny how life allows things to go wrong just days, weeks, or months after a large purchase that you simply could not afford. A better example would be buying a vehicle that runs well, and you can finance it because you have 5K in the bank plus 6 months' worth of your expenses and 2k for gas and maintenance. Build your credit with low debt-to-income ratios. You will be surprised at how much banks will finance your vehicles when

13

they see that your assets are much more than your debts. This way, when trouble comes, you keep your car, pay your bills, and keep your credit in good standing until trouble passes, however long that may be. To put it bluntly, credit is a vice for those who cannot wait and are impatient. There is no need for financing anything except your primary residence and investment properties that you either earn income from (rental) or plan to resale quickly, commonly referred to as house flipping.

  o   Low income - J.O.B. is just over broke.

Tying this into credit, if you feel as though you can afford a brand-new car with good credit on minimum wage, then you can do all the items within the chart and then some. Rethink your priorities and manage first the amount you have, then assess the amount you can borrow. Always keep borrowing under one-third of your income (except property). As a rule of thumb, save three times whatever it is that you want. So, you make minimum wage and are young, still with parents or grandparents, whether in or out of school. Ready to move out? Wait and consider the following things: if the average rent is $890 a month, do you have a minimum of $10,000 or $20,000 saved in your bank account right now? Do you have at least the foundation of the pyramid complete? Are you leaving for "peace of mind?" Why are you leaving unless you are being kicked out by Mom or Dad? Let's tackle the obvious; you have a minimum-wage job trying to get by until you can move out.

  ■   Base - $7.25 × 40hrs/wk. = $1160/month

■   Save - $116/month = $1392/yr.

■   Retirement - $174/month = $2088/yr.

■   Life / Hospital Income Insurance - $30/month = $360/yr.

■   Taxes - $151.30/month = $1,815.6/yr.

Remaining Balance - $688.70/month = $8264.40/yr.
For you to spend on bills and whatever else you want.

■   Growth - $290/month = $3,480/yr. (From Saving and Retirement)

All said and done; you will have more money than you have seen in the next 12 months of your life up to this point. Totaling it all up between your savings and your retirement account, you would have a total amount of $3,480 in total assets, and that does not include the interest that you earn on your retirement; if you factor that in, it would be $300 at a low 7% return. And with retirement, you want slow and steady, not aggressive. This is more than enough while living at home with parents or grandparents, but this is the project if you try to live off this on your own. For those who move out for peace of mind, the projects are not the most peaceful place. The lowest rent you will pay will place you in another room and another home with someone that does not love you or care about your problems; they only want the rent. Whereas at the rate in which you would be saving at home would, at a minimum, get out of your parent's house in 2 years. If you follow the steps precisely in two years, your total assets will end up being $11,739.77. If you were following your balance of $6,176.40 in your checking account, you would have a very well-maintained car that is something that you would be able to afford while living with Mom and Dad. Put aside $3,000, and none of that comes out of your retirement, savings, or life insurance, and with the total amount of assets that you will have now, this will be enough to look for a property for you to buy upon moving out as opposed to renting an apartment. You would be able to do all this with a minimum-wage job. There are multiple homeowners' programs available to help in a reasonable purchase. Reasonable means you do not have to empty your account on repairs, down payments, or anything else. However, you need to focus on your bi-weekly payment period of the $514.70 (after taxes) you bring home every other week. You may want to apply for a down payment assistance program that will help you keep your payments low; this being the first property, you may want to look for a condominium instead of a single-family home. This gives you the independence you want without the yard work, and the utilities are shared. It is a nice apartment-size dwelling, and while you are still earning minimum wage, it is a perfect starter home. This way, when/if your income increases, you can pay it off, put a renter in the condominium. This will add a positive stream of income, suggesting your earned income never increases. If you are thinking, "this is going to take forever." think again. If you are between the ages of 19 through 23 this entire process may take you only 3 years that's granted; you're staying at home until you purchase your condo, which means by the time you must get off your parent's health insurance, you're making passive income from your condo and looking for your new home and possibly a new car. So, let's recap by reprioritizing if we can turn $1,160 or $1,008.70 after taxes into $1,160 plus $500 to $900 per month in unearned income. Though $1500 to $2,000 per month is not a lot of money, you did this on minimum wage by just making the right decisions. Now your debt-to-income ratio is low, and your assets are growing rapidly.

○ Broken system - Recognize no system is perfect, and this is the best one that we have unless you want to leave the country and find out for sure.

This observation may be true on multiple levels; however, the process of fixing these problems does not start on the streets protesting. These problems are fixed in your pockets and your mind. Education is important but useless if not used. By first not being in the minimum wage category at all or at least not for long put your mind to work and not your body. Labor jobs are expendable and therefore not highly paid, while by putting your mind to work, you can double or even triple your wage. Degrees, certifications, and licenses can propel your wage to new heights. Remember, whether the system is with you or against you, you can do it with the right guidance and instruction, and the foundation method is a good start. It helps you branch out to different avenues that will open doors for you, hopefully, while you are still young. In summary: a healthy savings looks like 6 months to a year's worth of monthly income. During your younger years, life, disability, and hospital income policies, in total, are about $50 per month on average. As for retirement accounts, most companies have a retirement program and sometimes offer matching options. This is free money that should always be taken advantage of. Once the account is open, a healthy monthly contribution of 15% of your monthly income should suffice. This puts you in a great position for future financial endeavors. For the long-term, you will have your savings and retirement. Here, you also plan for your young or non-existent children's college fund, Health Plan, potential disabilities or illnesses, and life insurance.

Rethink your finances

List aside; this entire method is about being practical, intentional, and steadfast. Your financial future is not a sprint, and it is a marathon. A constant steady flow of good decision-making and well-thought-out delayed gratification. It is important to look at your entire financial picture and understand it. Most people are not still with Mom and Dad with no or low expenses. Some people live with their parents and still have expenses. Look at these expenses; every dime that goes out should not be haphazardly thrown; it should be strategically placed. In this method, it is important to always pay yourself first and never wait until after your expenses have come out and save whatever is left. (Spoiler alert: Nothing is ever leftover) If you make $100,000 per year and your expenses are $100,001 per year, then you are a dollar short every single year. The real question is why? This is an extreme example; however, most of us hover just over zero in our accounts. How much do you save? Do you make it a point to save every single month? Is your account growing every year? If not, how do you change that? There are simple steps that you can take to change these outcomes, the first being to write out a list of everything that comes out of your account or is supposed to come out of your account each month. These are going to be your monthly expenses. They should not fluctuate each month and should also not include discretionary expenses either; those should be reserved for the "everything else" section. You should make it a point to pay yourself first; this does not mean you have to get a large cut or that you must own your own business. This does not even mean that you must be rich, successful or where you want to be in life. This only means that if you make $1,000 a month, $2,000 a month, or even $4,000 a month, you understand that if you spend $1,000, $2,000, or $3,000 in expenses, you understand what you can afford to save, savings is the first step to financial competence. It is neither funny nor a joke that if your job stopped tomorrow or you decided that you were no longer a good fit for the company, you would be completely broke within days or weeks. This is a preventable outcome. Stretching yourself as far as you can stretch each month is not an effective way to create the savings that you need to get to where you would like to go in life. If you just graduated college and got your first job making $4,000 a month, it may be tempting to get a brand-new car today but wait. Delayed gratification is one of the most important concepts of being financially competent and able to withhold yourself from destroying your financial future. Yes, you have $4,000 in the bank at the end of the first month, but you do not have to run and leave Mom's house. Mom may have given you a few financial responsibilities, such as paying the light bill, the gas bill, or even your phone bill. However, this is okay; you do not have to leave the house yet. Write down all the income you have coming into your account and all the expenses you have coming out by printing out your bank statements and circle the negative numbers and highlight the positives. See exactly what you were spending in an average month, do this for 3 months at $2,000 a month, and within 3 months, you'll have $6,000. You may look and ask yourself, "now, what can I buy," remember, it has only been 3 months, talk to your financial advisor (i.e., an accountant, a banker, or someone in an investment firm) before you make big financial decisions. Consider most of these people are just trying to get you to spend money on a product or service that benefits them. Regardless, understand that they have knowledge that you can obtain to use for the betterment of your financial future. Ask questions about the options you have, and don't make quick decisions. It is important to stop and think about your income, think about your risk tolerance, and think about moving out and building your independence. Though you can go out and get approved for a $1,000 rent payment, why do it now? Doing something because you can, does not make you financially competent, it makes you financially incompetent and lacks self-control which takes no training at all. It also incapacitates you when trouble arises because of your lack of preparedness. Not to encourage that you struggle, though you make a reasonable amount of money, especially at an early age, rent is not developing you financially, it is developing someone else's financial future, one that was prepared and financially competent.

Look for vehicles that tend to run proficiently past 100,000 miles (not the new Mercedes), and look for something that you have three times the amount in your account to buy, plus gas for the entire year and the maintenance on top of that. Most importantly, always ensure you have at least 6 months' savings for your expenses before and after purchasing the vehicle. Organize your life in a format that will allow you to save, put towards retirement, and your life insurance because no matter how well you may be doing, life is one heartbeat away from ending. Do not rob your family of the peace of mind of being able to bury their child and loved one. The foundation is the most important part of the entire pyramid: it ensures that you can make it to the second tier and be able to build the future you see on TV. Nothing ever happened overnight. The flawless pictures that you come across were borne from a seed that they planted or their parents, watered, and grew into something that was worth reaping.

In rethinking your finances, consider the following:

- Save 10% of your monthly income in an account that is apart from your financial institution. Have your savings in a separate account and financial institution from your spending account.

- Put aside 15% of your income for retirement each month in a Roth IRA, traditional IRA, 401(k), Roth 401(k), 403(b), or other forms of retirement account that your financial advisor suggests after research and consulting at least two other advisors in other areas outside of banking, preferably a fiduciary which is a person who by law is required to put your interest above their own. Contribute to any employer plan that matches your contribution, then take the rest into a tax-free retirement plan. (Roth)

- Get a life insurance policy that you can afford and preferably one that does not increase over time. There are also Life Insurance strategies that can help you in retirement as well. Consult with a knowledgeable insurance agent or insurance broker that is familiar with such policies.

- Get health through your job if they provide it. Health insurance can immensely strain your finances if not provided through your job. Plan for health insurance early and apply for a policy that you must prove insurability. At a young age, most people do not have ailments that would cause them to be denied, and your rates will be much lower. Additionally, just because your job offers health insurance, they may not pay for it. This means that the amount of your premium is deducted from your paycheck. Check around to see if the amount deducted is the best you can find for the lowest price.

- Always have a date in mind for when you are going to reach tier two. Try not to push this off because it is the structure of your financial future.

- Remember that when you work hard, you can also play hard. Do not stress out over hitting these goals. Most of them are quite simple, and it is just a step in becoming financially competent.

- Lastly, always look for a person that can help in the arena of your finances you are struggling with. Do not just depend on Google or sources online; personal relationships are far more valuable.

You must pour the cement of your foundation with care but do not stress yourself out over it. The steps outlined here are simple to follow and even simpler to implement. Follow the steps in order, and put them in order of priority. It is appropriate to start one step and ask questions about another or start the process of another, given the timeframe of the task.

Example:

Jackie is a recent graduate student and has just started her first job using her degree in marketing. She is not sure if this will be the career she will stay in for the rest of her life, but the starting salary is decent. She moved away for college and renewed her lease since she found a job nearby. Her options are limitless, but her resources are not. Jackie has a frivolous lifestyle going out with friends throughout the week, as she is still young, single, and enjoys socializing.

Jackie could spend her money on anything she wants because she makes a $60,000 salary per year and her rent is only $1,000 for her studio apartment. Though she has $60,000 in student loans, she has made a payment plan of only $500 per month. Given her income is $5,000 per month and her bills are approximately $2,000 per month, she is living the dream. This is a common situation people face right after graduating, this massive jump in income is where the problems start. It starts small – purchase a new vehicle for $400 car note, insurance on it is $250, gas is $100 per month, start eating out more $600 per month, going out more (partying, drinking, shopping, etc.) $1,000 per month, start applying for credit cards for the "benefits and points" doing regular daily activities $500 per month with a bill for $50, upgrading cellphones $50 per month, and subscription services for $50 per month. $3,100; how did Jackie spend all her money plus $100? It happens all the time and until she decides to stop and evaluate, she is on the Titanic, sinking slowly. This is a story played out so often in our society because of the lack of financial competence.

Using the foundation method, Jackie would have never gotten to this point. Her foundation would be $500 in a savings account detached from her spending account in a separate institution, preferably a credit union, for the benefits down the road. She would also take her employer's match of 3% in her 401(k) plan; this is $150 from her and an additional $150 from the employer, totaling $300 per month. She would then invest up to the max in a Roth IRA of her own with an investment firm of $500 (the maximum contribution as of 2022 is $6,000 per year or $500 per month) which is 10% of her income and the rest, $100 would go into her 401(k) plan at work. Finally, she would purchase Life insurance and disability insurance for $50 per month.

- Saving - $500
- Retirement - $750 + Employer's $150 = $900
- Insurance - $50
- Total - $1,450
- Remainder - $1700 (Subtract employer contribution of $150)

Using the foundation method, Jackie still has $1,700 to spend on whatever she wants and can also start the process of home buying due to the extended nature of the purchase process. She also will have put away $16,800 in Savings and Retirement, with interest at 7%; she would have accumulated $1,368, making her total balance $18,168. This scenario is better than being stressed out and -$1,200 in debt after a year in the first scenario. The other difference is competence. One is financially competent, and the other is not.

With the right tools, anyone can succeed, and if you are having financial problems remember, you are not the problem, your plan is. Change your plan, and your problems will stop as well.

Building the Structure
Real Estate & Investments

Everyone "knows" how to be successful on paper, but few intimately understand how it works. "If only I had a million bucks, I'd..." a statement repeatedly said as if the million dollars is out of reach. Finances are like anything that can develop and improve over time. Practice makes perfect. If your uncle says, "I could have been a millionaire; here's how," the statement that follows is pure nonsense and should be ignored. The basis of that statement is flawed, suggesting he could have been rather than is on his way to becoming, which implies he does not understand the fundamentals of finances at all.

Imagine a ten-ton device that is the size of your house filled with huge vacuum tubes carrying information to and from different stations around the world within hours of that information being sent. This revolutionary device could transfer data remarkably fast, changing the face of our planet as we know it. If that sounds ridiculous, look up the first supercomputer. Everything I just said can be done much quicker and in the palm of your hands now in real-time, but you believe your uncle was the first person to think of it. Only if (so and so) was not on the same bus as him while he was talking about it, he would be the richest man on the planet right now. If you believe him, ask him a few follow-up questions if he is still alive. "Uncle, if you thought of it first, why didn't you pursue it at all? There are countless computer companies and cell phone companies, why didn't you even make a prototype or even end up in the electronics industry making the devices you claim to have thought up? You can get a patent with just drawings and the idea alone; do you even have a patent?" Inevitably all his delusions of grandeur will come crumbling down to the reality that these ideas did not stop at ideas; they were borne of challenging work, immense amounts of time, precise leadership, dedication, and sacrifice. They were not merely thoughts followed by rewards. Ideas nor knowledge lead to success; action does.

There are few lucky breaks in life, and the one's life brings are sometimes curses because if your foundation cannot sustain the increase, the luck will fall all the same. Everything worth having in life is a seed first planted, cultivated, watered, and harvested. If any of these stages are missed, the fruits of your labor will go unrewarded. Your uncle may have planted the seed, but the idea was dead anyway if he did not stick around to cultivate, water, or collect the harvest. He should be thankful that the idea came to fruition and that his laziness and inactivity did not keep the world from progressing.

There are countless stories of seaming blessings turning into bile. In the introduction, the statistics of how many go bankrupt within a few years after winning the lottery or receiving a windfall of money are astonishing. This is widely due to a significant lack of knowledge and inexperience in handling finances with just the little they had before the increase. Child star actors usually go off the deep end by their teen years and rarely come back. Dave Ramsey*, a finance radio host, often tells his story on the radio of his earlier years of real estate pursuits and how he amassed $4,000,000 in Real Estate Assets and $3,000,000 in Debts in mortgages on the properties giving him on paper a $1,000,000 Net Worth. This would be exciting for anyone in their early twenties; however, as he often says, he was "totally broke" because he had no liquid cash to his name and had over-leveraged his money. This was a huge problem that caused him to go bankrupt, almost costing his marriage and his sanity. This is a simple result of inexperience, emotional decision-making, and the inability to delay gratification that he still expresses to people from all levels of society to this day.

Rainy days are inevitable but are you a farmer or a bride? This may seem like a strange question because the two seem quite unrelated except for one correlation. The rain. A farmer patiently awaits rain while the bride plans everything down to the tee and absolutely dreads the rain. My wife and I made up this saying in our first year of marriage, this was our mantra to keep us focused on what is important and not the vagaries of life. When we first got married, I had recently started a business of drop-shipping items to people. I would sell products that I did not own online, and once they were purchased, I would buy them from a supplier and ship them to the purchaser. Theoretically, this was the perfect gig, and I was able to keep my job and still sell on the side. The first item I ever sold was a television; I was not sure if it was legitimate until I finally did it. This was monumental for me because, while at work, I made $350. A person agreed to buy a television from me for $500, and I only paid $150 to send it to them. I thought I had hit the jackpot. I made more that day than I had made the entire week of working at the job. I entered my credit card and sent the television right over to the person. I made a spreadsheet that day and started to list and sell all kinds of things to which I would find an extremely inexpensive supplier and then list those products on various sites such as Amazon, eBay, and other sites. In five months, I was averaging $5,000 per month, and within a year, I was averaging $7,000 a month. I continued to do this for about 2 years, the highest month being $12,000 in one month. I use my credit card to buy everything you can imagine under the sun. I thought it was a perfect plan because I had never used my money for anything. I sold products based on pictures, and once someone wanted them, they would purchase them. I would use my credit to supply those items to them, and it just seemed foolproof. Each month I would increase my credit limit just to make sure that I never would use my money ever again. I was well on my way to being a millionaire, and I turned my nose up at anyone who did not see that. I put in my two weeks' notice at my job, and shortly thereafter, they fired me. "Who cares," I thought, "I didn't need that job anyway." Embedded in me were two fundamental things, from my dad, I always remember that you should always have a job, and from my mom, I remembered that you should never be totally dependent on that job and that you should always have your own money on the side and don't be told what to do for the rest of your life. I left that job and went right into another one which was not a good one. However, psychologically I felt as though I had to get this opportunity because it was the one that was offered to me first. Between a bad job and debt racked up by the day, a rainy day was bound to come. However, I was the bride, everything had to be perfect, and Rain just was not on the itinerary. There were no seeds in the ground, and I was not waiting for any Harvest. Inevitably I lost that job as well due to my competing agendas, and I started to get sloppy with the business and ordered from any supplier I could find that was cheaper than another without checking to see the quality of these products. I received nothing but returns for 2 months straight. By this time, I had racked up over $19,000 worth of credit card debt alone. Of course, I also had a brand-new vehicle, and it was not too long since I signed a lease for a fancy apartment. I just asked my then-girlfriend and now wife to marry me. In a matter of 3 months from that day, I lost everything; I lost my car, my business, my job, and my apartment. My wife and I got married and had nothing. Young, married, and homeless. Luckily for me, my wife had a car, a 2001 Honda Civic. We spent the first two and a half years living with family members with no stability. One year after this humbling experience, I got an insurance sales representative job. We were determined never to be taken off guard again by the rain. No more loose ends, no more debt, and no more shortcuts. We spent the next year-and-a-half working hard to purchase our first home. During this year and a half, I never made more than $30,000, and my credit score hovered around 540. Using the programs that I will mention later in this chapter, I had a 560-credit score and $3,000 to my name when we closed. However, we were debt-free except for student loans and the mortgage. Within three years, we were able to open our own insurance agency and are now well on our way to Financial Freedom. Rain will always come, but if you are a bride living your life on the edge, your dress will be ruined, your makeup will run, the venue will not reschedule, and you are setting yourself up for failure. However, if you are the farmer, the rain will come, and you will rejoice because the fruits of your labor will be rewarded.

The structure is the next part of the pyramid, where the foundation takes you. Real Estate and Investments can be one and the same but should be seen as two sides of the same coin and will be used in tandem with each other if worked correctly. Both are equally important parts of the equation, and fundamentally they are the same; however, they are separate paths, and no matter how well you understand the concepts of either, you must focus on one to master its full potential. Real Estate is a full-time or part-time job which means it requires 4-8 hrs. per day of our time to be sustainably successful. Can you spend less time on this and get lucky occasionally? However, when building a foundation, sustainability is key, and consistency is how firm structures with sustainable futures are made.

Investments are a continuation of your retirement plan. This is when you have set up your retirement plan, preferably at your job and outside of work as well, to ensure you are able to diversify your assets and learn how your portfolio performs, observing its growth and losses over time. After doing this for some time, you will have a good grasp of how this process works and how the peaks and troughs make you feel, this will allow you to aim your sights at what interests you the most and what you want to focus your investments on for the long run. Investments is a very broad term that is misunderstood and misused in a variety of ways, from "I need to *invest* in some new clothes" to "I need to reallocate some of my *investments* to mid-cap mutual funds to offset my high-risk analysis per our last annual review" to even "I'm an investor of short-term *investments* such as options trading, penny stocks, cryptocurrency, and forex." The reality is there are many connotations associated with the term; however, the definition is "the act of laying out money or capital in an enterprise with the expectation of profit or the purchase of an asset or item acquired with the goal of generating income or appreciation."

Though you may feel you "deserve" to get a new outfit or car, these items, no matter how much you want them, and make excuses for them, referring to them as "investments for your happiness," are not investments. Items purchased for your own consumption are very rarely investments at all and do not lead to happiness in most cases, either. Many studies confirm that buying material things do not make us happy; they usually result in temporary joy, but this state rarely lasts more than a few days. The reality is our brain is filled with receptors that are more stimulated in the wanting process and not so stimulated in the getting process. For this reason, it is important that our foundation of investing is set up for the long run and not for temporal gains, as is the case with penny stocks, cryptocurrency, option trading, and forex. There is nothing wrong with these, but these are not investments, they are day trading which is a respectable part-time or full-time profession. However, as in the case of real estate, these hours must be fulfilled to get the total benefit from this. If not, this too will lead to ruin. Investing is a long-term commitment to your future.

The Structure is the Framework
-Before getting to the structure, you should have at least attained the following goals.
- Have a minimum of 6 months' worth of expenses saved and put aside as an emergency fund.
  - Preferably put this in a separate savings account that is not your main savings.
  - Emergency fund is not to be touched unless you are missing the three most important needs.
    - Food/ Water
    - Health

■   Shelter

o   Notice car repairs, cell phone bills, cable, internet, or even electric or gas bills are not included in the emergency fund account.

o   Though you may feel as though you cannot live without these things, they are not a matter of life and death; at the point in which you have the provision of a job, passive income, or business generating an income, you can sustain yourself again, such extras can be attained quite readily.

o   Rather than depending on your emergency fund for menial things, have a personal savings account in your primary financial institution.

o   Saving at least 1% of your monthly income to take care of short-term goals in the Everything Else category.

o   This saving account will fluctuate depending on the demand at the time.

o   In general, be slow to spend and save at a minimum of two times the object or thing trying to be obtained.

Example:

■ $10,000 Car, save $20,000, then buy it cash or finance it to build credit without stressing the fear of default or repossession.

■ $2,000 Vacation, save $4,000 and keep your savings growing while having fun.

- Pay attention to your retirement account, diversify your portfolio, and see which stocks/bonds/ETFs/hedge funds/mutual funds perform and which do not.
  - During the time it takes for you to get your savings accounts together, you should be watching your retirement account like a hawk.
  - Preferably place investments in a spreadsheet and watch to see their individual growths and losses.
  - At a minimum, check this yearly and eliminate investments not performing or costing you consecutive years in a row.
  - Watch the news and keep up with companies you have invested in.
  - This is the groundwork for doing well in the Structure part of investing.
  - The goal in retirement is to grow at a steady pace. 7% - 9% is great, it is not so much about having high returns so much as it is about having steady returns.
  - The benefit will start to increase as the sheer number increases.

Example:
  - 7% return on $600 is $42
  - 7% return on $100,000 is $7,000.
  - Imagine earning an extra $583.33 per month from a $100,000 principle.

Maneuvering into the structure.

    1.   Real estate, this is the biggest investment most people ever get into. This should not be taken for granted, nor should it be avoided. It is an important aspect to note that if you are going to pay monthly for your shelter, you should at least end up owning it and building equity. Rather than struggling along the way and looking for apartments, take this alternate route instead. Search for a trustworthy real estate agent; though this may seem like a leap out of faith, you would be surprised at the skills that they have that may help you get into your first home. They tend to have tricks up their sleeve that can help you achieve this goal quicker than you may think. There are programs and grants out there that they may know about that sometimes come with little to no down payment. A good Agent would readily find these credits, programs, or grants for you to get you into the home of your dream. Unlike the US average for a home, you can find a home in any area that you like for almost any price; you would be surprised. A great program that is out is called The Neighborhood Assistance Corporation of America ("NACA"), which is a non-profit, community advocacy and homeownership organization helping low-income and poor credit applicants get into homes with no closing cost. Homeownership can be done without you having the career that you want at this

time. Though homeownership is a goal for this portion of the Structure, it is not the only portion this section covers. Real estate goes far beyond you becoming a homeowner. It ventures into you owning property that earns you passive income in several ways.

      a.   Multi-family
           i.   Duplex
          ii.   Triplex
        iii.   Apartment
      b.   Multipurpose home
           i.   Home attached to a business
          ii.   Business in property
      c.   Apartment complex
      d.   Single-family home
      e.   Commercial property
           i.   Office building
          ii.   Warehouse
        iii.   Strip mall
         iv.   Lounge
          v.   Restaurant

If you were wondering what people mean when they say they have passive income or unearned income. Real Estate is one of the ways that you can have passive or unearned income. If you purchase your first property as a multi-family home and have renters in the other units, you may not only not have a mortgage payment after their rents are paid, but you may also have leftovers to put in your own pocket. This is a method known as house-hacking. Commonly used for your first property due to all the incentives offered to first-time home buyers. All the incentives and programs can be combined and used to your advantage. Once you are ready to leave and get your single-family home of your dreams, you can put a renter in the unit that you were living in and have them pay for your new mortgage on the home that you wanted. You can do this if you have a plan.

Example:

- Purchase a duplex for $100K with a 3.5% interest rate; your payments will be $449.04 plus taxes and insurance, $1,200 each per year, for a total payment of $649.04.
- If you charge rent of $900, not only will your renter pay your mortgage, but they will also pay most of your utilities.
- Therefore, if you make minimum wage, almost 100% of your check will go into your pocket, which you can save and get the car you want cash and invest the rest.

2. Investments, these are investments outside of just owning real estate. This book is merely a guide to getting your feet wet in Investments. It is important that you note this is not a guide that will tell you what some

of the best investments to go with or even some of the best products that are offered. It is merely to get you to the level where you can generate passive income outside of your job.

Cash flow is the money you work for, and it is your time invested that gives you a return. This is how investing in the stock market works. You get out of it what you put into it; however, instead of you investing time for money, you are investing money for money. If you spend a lot of time and effort learning different trends and watching how the market changes, you will develop skills that will allow you to earn a sizable return. Typically, the initial goal or reason for investing is to meet the needs of your expenses. The more efficient you are at investing and the more capital there is to work with, the greater the returns and the better off you are. Once again though the potential in investing is great, the risks are still there as well. Keep this in mind when you see large returns; there are also large losses. The earlier you get started, as in your age, the riskier you can manage to be; however, as you grow older and get closer to your retirement age, it is wise to become more conservative. The point of this is not for you to complete the foundation, purchase your first home or property, and lose it all in the market. It is to find and keep advisors around you; if you have someone who helps you with your retirement account, this person would also be efficient in Investments and may have a good idea of how to guide you in your investment endeavors. Remember to take your time and move slowly, thinking first and not acting first. The quicker you act, the more you must react, and the more you think, the more proactive you can be. Never be a quick sale; always try to be a quick study and learn from your advisors the best options on the table and choose them according to your needs at the time. The goal initially should be to fund your investments. Once you have your savings together, you treat this account as if it is an additional savings, whereas you put most of your extra income in your investment account. Then when you hit a certain level, as far as principal, in your account, there are a lot of things you can do to grow it from there. Initially, do not start off aggressively until you understand how the market works, how it affects your income, and how it will work out for you overall, slow and steady. It is better for you to get to a goal of $50,000 having only put $30,000 into the account and let that amount accumulate interest at a steady pace rather than to put away $50,000 into an account and have losses along the way and only have $30,000 to show for it. Initially, you just want to put money into the account and let it grow at a very steady pace. Once you have hit whatever goal you set for yourself, then you can diversify your portfolio, splitting it into aggressive, moderate, and conservative sections. You may even have a section of your portfolio dedicated to extremely risky investments. This is not so harmful if your entire account is at $50,000 and only $5,000 is used for extremely risky investments. Whereas, if you have only $5,000 in the entire account, then having that entire amount extremely risky, which has not only large returns but also large losses as well, may be counterproductive for your development. Once you have completed the foundation, which means you have an emergency fund in place, you also have a side savings account for short-term goals that you are continually depositing small amounts of your income into, you have your retirement account set up and steadily growing, and life and health insurance with any other insurances that protect your assets; you may feel as though you can be extremely risky. Remember, the entire point of this structure is to be steady and stable. Having sustainable growth is better than having large payouts with large consequences.

Interest is great, growing your principle and net worth, but dividends are what provides income. Different investment types offer dividends, such as Stocks, Mutual Funds, ETFs, and REITs. The amount varies vastly, but as you are learning about the investments you would like to invest in, dividends are an important factor you will want to consider when making your decision. There are two main ways to receive your dividend payout. You can either receive them as a cash payout, however frequently they get distributed, or you can reinvest them automatically. There is no right or wrong answer, but the wisest option is both. Although you are not set into any one decision for life, the best practice is to reinvest them early on until you have a sizeable principle and later receive cash payouts.

Example:

Michael started investing directly after starting his first job while in high school at a local retail store. He has set up his foundation, and after just 3 short months, he was ready to invest and prepare for homeownership when he graduates. There is no set amount to how much you would like to invest; it is entirely based on individual comfort level. Since Michael lives at home with his family, he does not need most of his income. His comfort level is $100 per month for now. He wants to earn $100 per month in dividends as a starting goal. Michael feels comfortable investing in stocks that have a 3% dividend payout. He will need to have a $40,000 principle to accomplish his goal. He takes the first 6 months to learn how the market works and which stocks he would like to stick with. Once the 6 months have passed, he will need to increase the amount he invests in reaching his goal in five years. Given his current living situation, he has elected to only keep 10% of his income and invest the rest in meeting his goal. He recognizes that this is the best time in his life and possibly the only time he will be able to invest this much of his income with impunity. $100 may not seem sufficient, but Michael does not have to work for this income at all, it is money-earning money, which is passive income. Michael studies the market and has his portfolio diversified in such a way that he averages a 7% return on his total investments. He receives a 3% dividend on top of that, which he reinvests while in school. Over the summer, Michael increases his working hours, doubling his income which he still invests 90% of. The 10% has also doubled, allowing him to purchase more of what he likes and clothes for school the following year. Due to all his diligent efforts, Michael reached his goal in four years, which was also the year he graduated, allowing him to use his principle as a down payment to purchase his first property, which was a duplex. He currently rents the other half and pays no mortgage due to his tenant's next door. As Michael progresses through life, he makes higher and higher goals to increase his passive income.

This example just shows the better your foundation, the better you are equipped to take advantage of the next economic downturn (i.e., Buy Property) or benefit from the next investment explosion. You may be thinking, he saved up all that money only to put it into a home, so was it worth it? Anyone can get approved for a home loan, there are programs for down payment assistance and other grants/incentives as well. Arguably, a fellow classmate of his could have partied and played video games each summer and throughout the year, gotten approved through a program, and did the same thing. Working harder does not beat working smarter. I would agree 100% with that argument if Michael, in this example, were somehow excluded from doing both for some reason. The example shows not only the diligence of a young man charting his financial future, but it also shows the financial competence he demonstrated with his calculated decisions pushing him ahead. Though someone else could do the same or close to the same if said person has the financial prowess to navigate the feats in the example without the time and effort Michael invested in over his 4 years of high school being slim to none. This goes back to Chapter 1, which talks about the time and effort needed to set up a sustainable foundation for your own financial goals. Without foundation, everyone would anticipate the building's collapse. The other student would not have the discipline, skills, or knowledge to sustain this for long, if at all. You cannot skip steps and expect fruitful results. In fact, there are statements and arguments made like this all the time. Though these philosophies and speculations around this topic work in a thought bubble, they do not work in the real world where a person's habits lead people down one of three paths, average (majority), neither increasing nor decreasing in life, failure (about 20%) spiraling downward, and success (about 20%) progressing forward using life experiences of themselves and other people to reach and exceed their goals. Once your foundation is in place, you can expand your options and still move ahead. This is also referred to as the 20/60/20 rule in finance.

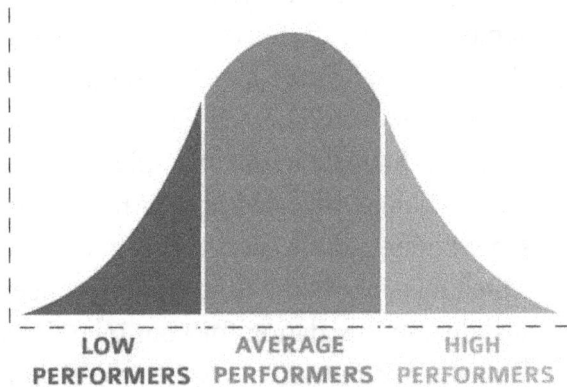

	LOW	AVERAGE	HIGH
	PERFORMERS	PERFORMERS	PERFORMERS

Example:

You work in retail, earning $10/hr. 25 hours per week while you are in college.

Cash flow: $1,000/month

Assets: Saving, Retirement, and Life Insurance totaling $275/month. (Save $100, Retire $150, and Insurance $25)

Expenses: Food, cell phone bill, and gas for your car or bus fare totaling $600/month

Liabilities: Credit Card totaling $25/month with a total balance of $300

This leaves you with $100 to blow. However, while in school, you can cut back on most things that you will need when you get your life started. You can do one of the following things each month:

1.   spend the $100
2.   save the $100
3.   invest the entire $100
4.   payoff debt with $100, then save $50 and invest $50
5.   do a combination of the 4 items, save $25, invest $25, spend $25, and pay off debt $25.

All these following options come with vastly different outcomes, and the outcome is what I would like to focus on. Suggesting you are at a four-year Institution, the option's outcomes are as follows:

1.   With this option, you would have accumulated a lot of stuff with little to no value at the end of your four years.

2.   In this option, you would have saved an additional $4,800 at the end of your four years.

3.   In this option, you would have invested $4,800, and with a 7% average return on your investment, you would have accumulated $727.86 totaling $5,527.86 at the end of your 4-year college career.

4.   With this option, you would have paid off your credit card in 3 months. You would have saved up $2,250 and invested $2,250 at a 7% return; you would have accumulated $2,598.09, and you will have gained an extra $25 in your budget from paying off debt to spend on extras. Totaling $4,848.09 in assets

5.   With this option, you will have saved $1,200, invested $1,200 at 7% earning $181.97 in interest totaling $1,381.97, spent $1,200, and paid off your debt in 6 months, giving you an extra $50 to spend. Total assets – $2,581.97 after 4-years of college.

Obviously, in terms of net worth, option three would be the best option; however, you determine what works for you. The benefit of the foundation is that in all these options, you would have saved at least $4,800, your retirement account would have accumulated at a 7% average return of $8,291.79, give or take, and even your life insurance would have accumulated cash value of

$10-$15. It would only add to the numbers if you invested during this time as well. This is just one of the multiple examples out there. The goal is to change the way you act. Your actions are a habit, and habits produce both good and bad fruits. By making saving, investing, and protecting a habit, you will always have what you need and will continue to stay on track with your finances. This example only takes into consideration the extra amount of money you get to allocate, not the asset allocation, which is the first thing you allocate before expenses. This means that whichever option you choose, you will still have access to the amounts listed above of $4,800 in saving in your long-term savings account and $8,291.79 in your retirement account.

The Frameworks of the Structure

The key to success is the simple consistencies built into the foundation. Once you have mastered this, you are able to tackle the walls that make up your structure. The first wall is Cash Flow, for the purposes of this book, we will only focus on the active or earned income. The following book will dive into passive and portfolio cash flow; however, cash flow is the income you work for now. Secondly, Expenses are the things you pay for regularly. Thirdly, Assets, which are things that pay you without you having to work for them. This ranges vastly though the general idea stays the same, you trade money for money. In most cases, there is still an amount of time invested as well, especially in the case of rental property, subscribers, royalties, and business. These all require an initial investment of time and knowledge (reading). Finally, Liabilities which are things that cost you money, usually for a set duration. The differences between liabilities and expenses are:

• Liabilities can become assets or cash flow with the preparation and utilization – A home you own and live in with a mortgage is a liability, if you move out and rent it out, that same home with a mortgage would be an asset to you. A car you drive, and finance is a liability to you. If you drive for Door Dash or Lyft in your car now, it is cash flow.

• Liabilities have a set beginning and an end date, and expenses are forever. The good thing about that is once you have passively met the needs for your expenses, you can retire once your liabilities are paid off.

• Expenses are discretionary, and though you may feel you have to pay a certain amount on bills, there are always other options. Never relinquish your control to the elements of your life. You do not have to be with the company you are with that you feel is overcharging you or mistreating you.

• Expenses offer no financial benefit to you, "buy this and save!" is a lie. Unless you are purchasing an asset, you are not saving or investing. With that, spend your money on expenses that complement you and benefit you personally without breaking the bank.

Listed below are these items broken down:

a.   Cash flow
  i. Job
 ii. Business
iii. Hobby (with pay)
	b. Expenses
	   i. Food
	  ii. Utilities
	 iii. Bills
	 iv. Insurance
	  v. Clothes
	 vi. Misc.

c.   Assets
   i. Rental property
  ii. Stocks
 iii. Bonds
 iv. ETF's
  v. Mutual Funds
 vi. Subscribers
vii. Royalties
viii. Business
	d. Liabilities
	   i. Debt
	     • Car note
	     • Mortgage
	     • Loans
	     • Credit Cards
	  ii. Dependents
	     • Children
	     • Family members depending on you
	     • Pets
	 iii. Law
	     • Taxes
	     • Lawsuits
	     • Tickets
	     • Fines

Income Vs. Expense Table

Joist the structure to the foundation

Keeping the fundamentals is important for the stability of the structure. Though tempting to lax standards set forth in the foundation, continue to maintain these foundational habits, as they are key to moving up the pyramid. These are foundational for a reason, and foundations hold up the structure and beyond. If a home or building is being erected and the foundation gets a crack in it, the foundation must be repaired, if fixable, and completely replaced, if significantly damaged. Financially speaking, this would be like discontinuing savings or retirement plans while in the process of purchasing a home. That would be a crack in the financial foundation, especially if you discontinued these habits to purchase above your affordability (i.e., above 30% of your income). The steps only work if followed and maintained in order, or else, they will not work. Jeff Olson, in his book *The Slight Edge**, said it best, "As I began to examine my successes and failures, what I gradually realized was that the very same activities that had rescued me from failure... would also rescue me from average and carry me from the survival line to the success line – *if I would just keep doing them.*" The same things that brought success before are the same things that will bring success in the present and the future. So stay the course and continue maintaining the foundation. Gradually progress with feet planted firmly on the ground before progressing forward.

As I mentioned in the previous chapter how I lost everything. My blunder was due to an unstable footing on the ground. Though my effort continued, had I saved 10% of my earnings, invested 15% in a Roth IRA, and purchased health insurance, hospital indemnity, and disability insurance, I would be sitting in a different position right now. Though I am proud of where I have come, it was not without self-inflicted setbacks. I had no business using credit for the business I was working and no business with a $481 car note on a Toyota Camry. Do not repeat my mistakes; build a solid foundation and stick to it. Do not go into debt unnecessarily, if you do not have it in your bank account, you do not have it. Place your foundation and build your structure, buy property within 30% of your income and invest in businesses you believe with in only an amount you can afford to lose.

Shelter Covering
Everything Else

    As your foundational structure comes to its completion, there are some things to be mindful of. Take the habit-forming steps from early in this book as a guide towards financial success but do not mistake these building blocks as foolproof. A house or structure is susceptible to the elements and harsh realities of life without a roof on the building. You are the same way, as stated before, simply knowing how to do something does not constitute an understanding of what you are doing.

    When you tell a child not to touch the oven, he may listen to you and not touch it. He may go through his entire childhood without touching an oven because he follows this instruction. But is this optimal? Will this child grow up with the idea that he should not touch the oven because only women cook in the kitchen? Will he become a rugged traditionalist who does not know how to cook or refuses to learn because it is not his place? This is what following instructions with no understanding does.

    Telling someone to do this or that with your money is pointless without understanding in most cases because they do not form the right actions in the eye of a storm. "Don't get into debt; it's bad for you," your parents say. Credit card companies relentlessly market to you OPM (Other People's Money), showing your favorite celebrity using credit, "we can get you out of a tight spot," "don't you want stuff you can't afford? We can help you with that." Who do you think will win when the tide changes? Which voice will you listen to? The one you heard in passing once or twice in your life or the one that's marketing to you, on all your favorite shows and movies, on your phone, in ads online, billboards, mail, banks, and shhh.... Your hypocritical parents, too, are not by what they say but by what you see them do. All these cues say, "in case of an emergency, use credit," and just like that, you are trapped. Like a fly in a spider's web, the lender closes in on you to suck you dry for the next 3-5 or 6-10 years of your life. Were 5 years worth an item you could have saved up for in a matter of weeks or months? There goes that voice again, "you can have it now, though."

The moral is to continue educating yourself and stay committed to the process. Knowing is good, Doing is Great, but Understanding is life-changing. Once you understand your finances on a fundamental level, you will start to grow and grow sustainably. OPM (Other People's Money) has been sold to many as the way to quick success and riches. However, using the same acronym and changing the meaning of the letters is truly the way to succeed and have financial freedom.

Optimize, Protect, and Maximize (OPM)

Optimizing is getting the most out of your finances as they stand now. If you work a minimum wage job now, practice saving that 10% saving on the first block of the pyramid. Utilize your company's retirement plan and start putting away 1% of your income into the retirement section of your income in an outside retirement account and build up until you can get your contribution to 15% between your job and your outside funds. Increase the percentage every quarter of the year until your goal is reached. Then, start slowing to make your growth sustainable.

Protect your finances from unnecessary loss and significant setbacks. It is extremely hard to save if every time you save a considerable sum, something inevitably happens that causes you to have to start over. This is preventable by maintenance, insurance, and time. Though, when you have a goal that you are trying to reach, it is hard not to save as much as you can and ignore maintenance, let your insurance lapse, or convince yourself that this "thing" just cannot wait. This is a gap in understanding that allows you to believe that you can save $10,000 per year and ignore your car's check engine light on, not get a $20 hospital income policy, or get a larger-than-expected check that just must go to something. Protection is particularly important and should not be ignored. A stop loss on investment could be the difference between a recession placing you in financial ruin or on the path to financial surplus. Being intentional about protecting your hard-earned money is a great sign of wisdom and puts you further along your path to success.

Maximizing is making the most income you can at your job and/or business with your investments, rental income, and other income opportunities. The way to maximize your income to its fullest potential is to first learn about your income. If you are indeed at a minimum-wage job right now, you have two options, seek growth opportunities within your company or leave the company for higher-paying job opportunities. However, when making this transition, you do not want to put the carriage before the horse, meaning do not leave your job before you have another opportunity. It is much easier to get a job when you have a job than when you do not have one. Also, weigh your options. As income goes up, mental work and problem-solving do as well.

Daymond John* tells of his rise to success by waiting tables while his clothes-designing business was getting off the ground. He worked extremely hard to have the best customer service and never let himself get overconfident or arrogant. He did not need to tell his boss and co-workers that he was going to the top, he just let the results show for themselves. He says that he waited tables even as his brand Fubu was getting million-dollar contracts and rarely called out for work or missed days until it began to cost him money to continue working at the restaurant rather than going all into his business.

This story just goes to show that maximizing income does not always mean going out and getting a higher-paying job which also costs you more mental capacity. Instead, it shows that you can work a low-income job that is less mentally taxing to allow you to use your mind on your own outside financial endeavors as such side businesses and hobbies, real estate investing, day trading, secondary jobs, or even internships, furthering your education and learning a new language. The latter may not seem income generating, but these will make the greatest change in your mindset, which further deepens your capacity to grow financially in the future.

Sealing in the Ceiling.

- This is the "everything else" or ceiling. This holds it together, keeping the weather out (unprofitable habits) as well as financial hardship strains that are avoidable. This portion heavily relies on the structure and is achieved once the flame is built.

• The ceiling is reached at the point in which the frame of the structure is completed. Nothing fancy, just the basics.
• The foundation should be solidified.
  ○ At this point, we are proficient at saving a minimum of 10% of your cash flow per month.
  ○ Also, 15% of your cash flow should be put towards retirement.
  ○ Lastly, your life and health insurance should always be active and in place.
• The structure frame should be built.

    ○   At a minimum, you should have purchased some form of Real Estate in lieu of renting.

    ○   You should have at least a rudimentary understanding of Investments.

• The "everything else" portion is an extension of everything that we have covered up until now.

<u>Insulating the Attic.</u>

1.   Venturing into the "everything else" portion, we should be thinking rather than acting first. At this point in time, your understanding of your finances should be prevalent, and the desire for depreciating assets should have diminished. However, everything else does include menial things that we have been building up to guiltlessly splurge now that we have a foundation and a structure. The goal from henceforth is just to maintain the growth that you have, of course, to continue saving at a faster rate if you deem it necessary, also continue to find your retirement account, and keep your life and health insurance. By this time, you should be enjoying your real estate property and planning to purchase others in the future for the purpose of financial gain. Lastly, your pursuits in investing should be at a point just above a novice, and with the help of your financial advisor, you will begin to see the increase.

2.   Financial competence should be obtained.

- Finance - The management of money, credit, banking, and investments.
- Competence - The quality of being adequately or qualified physically and intellectually.
- Putting these two terms together means the quality of being adequate or well-qualified intellectually to manage money, credit, banking affairs, and investments. This is the goal at the point in which you have reached the ceiling. It is not to constantly put you down and the desires you have, but to mold your thought process when engaging in such endeavors.

Example:

You have graduated from college with a bachelor's degree in marketing, and you are looking for a career with benefits as well as a reasonable wage.

With the skills from the foundation method, some of the thoughts you may have when offered a position are:

How much will I be able to save? (Saving)

Will this include a retirement plan? (Retirement)

Will it also include life insurance and health insurance? (Insurance)

What stocks are the retirement accounts that they offer invested in? (Investment)

How much would I be able to finance a new property now and rent it out for passive income? (Real Estate)

How much extra will I have after all expenses are met? (Everything Else)

This example was not to go over numbers or math but to demonstrate how your thinking should be set up to make better financial decisions that would deem you financially competent. This example focuses on questions on the foundation first, then the structure, and lastly, the "everything else." The first three question stands for the most important aspects as it pertains to the job in which you are accepting. The next two questions are the second most important quality of the position. Lastly, the final question is the benefit of having a job. As you may have figured out by now, first 3 questions are the foundation, second 2 questions are the structure, and last question is the ceiling. If you structure your finances this way, then your sacrifice will be rewarded repeatedly.

Continual Finances

Fasteners
Bills, liabilities, and debt. **< Finances Books / Financial Planner**
Stuff and Things. **< Your Imagination**

Plumbing
Losses, Emergencies, Misfortune. Overspending, Under Budgeting, and Large Unnecessary Expenses. **< Insurance Agent / Financial Advisor / Attorney**

Electrical wiring
Income, Cash Flow, Dividends, and ROI. **< Real Estate Consultant / Investment Advisor**

Nails & Screws
Bills, liabilities, and debt. Stuff and Things.

As part of any structure, there must be something holding it together. These are, oftentimes, hidden beneath the surface and never thought about until you are ready to change something structural, like removing a wall or adding fixtures and upgrades. Finances are the same way they are put aside and set on autopilot until you decide to change them. Before changes are made, however, oftentimes fasteners are showing in the screws, and nails of life are seen by onlookers and passersby. In finance, fasteners are bills, liabilities, and debt. When you initially start paying bills, no one sees them, your friends and family members do not care about each other's bills, but once you lose your ability to pay for them and need help, that is when your nails start to show. This is the first sign that something needs to change. This is an indicator that it might be time to make some changes in your financial life. This section breaks down bills, liabilities, and debt into digestible chunks that makes your success inevitable and failure improvable. Life can only be understood from past experiences; however, you can learn from others' experiences rather than living them out yourself.

1

Financial Competence: Part 2

Kiana called the office for the fifth time this week, she was overdue for her car insurance payment, and this was the last day she had to pay before it lapsed, and she would have a fine from the state or worse, an accident that would not be covered. She did not have the money in her account to pay, but she called her agent anyway to explain that she would have it by her next paycheck on Friday. This was Kiana's 13th late pay, and there were no exceptions after 12 consecutive non-pays. She was going to be canceled, and she did not know what to do. The agent explained the situation and let her know that if she did not get a payment by the end of the day, she would have to go without insurance for an entire week until her paycheck came in. Kiana got off the phone and, in a frenzy, she called all her friends and family to see if she could borrow the money; she needed to make her payment that day and keep her policy active. Everyone knew why she was calling and did not answer her call, this was not her first time calling for money, and it would not be the last if she kept doing things the way she was. She reached into her purse to find any credit card she could that had the smallest balance on it so that she could pay something on her insurance and hopefully keep it active. Not knowing, she went online to try to make a payment with any of her credit cards, she tried every card in her purse, and one after the other, they declined. She started calling more distant "friends," the ones who would want favors (not monetary), for allowing her to borrow the money even for a brief period. Not even they would answer her cries, except for Jeffrey. Jeffrey was aggressive, short-tempered, and very messy, he wanted payment from her as soon as possible if he made this arrangement on her behalf. She rushed over to his house to "pay" for him to loan her the money. After "payment," he decides he will not pay her bill after all and tells her to get out of his house and that her insurance bill is not his problem; it is hers. After trying everything she could, Kiana was completely out of options after giving even her body. She could not get another line of credit, title loan, or anything to pay that day. She never called the insurance agent back and just tried to get a quote online to see if she could get some cheap insurance to keep her from getting fined by the state, getting forced insurance by her lien company, or God forbid, getting into an accident. Every quote that she got was extremely high; therefore, she just waited until her paycheck. She had to go to work, so she took her chances driving every day until Thursday of the following week. She was pulled over by a state patrol officer, her car was towed, she was fined, and now she was in Jeopardy for losing her job. She called the insurance agent to see what she could do to get her insurance started again, to which he firmly responded that payment would be required to get the insurance started again. Kiana, now without a car, her dignity and respect, and no money finds herself stuck in the pile of life's troubles. With nowhere to run anymore, she must look at her life and see the reality that her finances controlled her life and not the other way around.

With this newfound realization, she has two options to go forward in her life, and these options will determine her future outcome. She can either choose to take responsibility for the problems that she has created in her life and successfully plan to get herself out of this reality, or she can choose to deflect the blame of this immense problem onto society, friends and family, God, or any other scapegoat she could find. If she chooses the latter, she will continue to find herself in more debt, obtain more liabilities, and continue to fall behind on her bills. Suppose it was not her fault that she got herself into this. In that case, she has no responsibility or the ability to get herself out of it and is therefore subject to every negative and positive outcome that her life brings her. However, if she chooses to take full responsibility for her life, she has the power to change everything. This is the only way she can change anything in her life.

Blaming only gives the key to your freedom to someone else but taking responsibility gives you the key to your own freedom and allows you to make decisions that will enhance your life and give you power over your problems. Kiana was faced with this crossroads, as everyone must face. Not that everyone will be faced with liabilities or debt in their lives, but everyone has bills and responsibilities that they must take care of, and without the proper outlook on these obstacles, financial freedom is out of reach. But with the right perspective, you can take full control of this problem(s) and your very own hands will resolve it. Looking at Kiana's problems, she did not lack effort, she also worked extremely hard to try to resolve this; however, efforts and diligent work alone do not resolve problems. There are a lot of hard workers that have more problems than they have years left on this Earth to work. Therefore, these people are forced to retire later and, in some cases, not at all. They work arduously until the day they die. Everyone has problems in their lives, but if you choose to blame someone else or ignore them, time is very unforgiving. However, if you take responsibility and fasten your life with the tools of resolution and long-term sustainable plans, your efforts and arduous work will not go in vain. Directly following the lesson below, produce some solutions to Kiana's problem. Once you have read this section, produce an action plan for her to take, and on the following page, there will be one of those potential resolutions that you may have produced. There are no 100% correct answers for how Kiana could get out of her problems however taking responsibility, putting thought into the outcome, and applying the concepts of financial competence; she can chart a plan that will delay gratification and line her obstacles in a row and conquer them one by one, she too will have success in her life.

Every building has nails and screws.

Nails are an intricate part of a building structure; it is what holds everything together. These consist of bills, liabilities, and debt.

    1.   Bills

- Bills are not something we have the option of opting out of; they are continuous and will always be there. No one is above bills, although there are some that seem to not have them; however, they simply choose not to let them hurt them.
- Bills are not an elaborate enigma but a number, most of the time a consistent one. Remember to always have this number memorized to ensure you do not spend them on stuff or things.
- Bills are, in some cases, subjective based on priorities, not everything you buy deserves a column or row on a spreadsheet.

Examples:

   ○ Personal grooming services, I.e., Barbershop, hair salons, manicure/pedicure, waxing, and eyebrows.
   ○ Cable TV, movies, entertainment (arcade, sports events/games, and eating out)
   ○ Going to the bar, lounging with friends, and social events.

- Most bills are not subjective and are a must-have; these are the bills that should be written down and memorized.
   ○ Rent/mortgage
   ○ Water bill
   ○ Electric bill

o   Gas bill

o   Grocery bill (some items may be subjective, take note of only the ones that are essential)

o   Insurance bill (Auto, Fire, I.e. (Homeowners or Renters), Life, Health)

o   Foundation (note that these are not conventional bills; however, this is how you should look at it, as a bill. Meaning you do not give it an option.)

- Savings deposits
- Retirement investments

- All of these will make up a number; this number usually is consistent because, as humans, we are creatures of habit. Note the following before you spend your money on subjective bills, stuff, or things.

Example:

o   Rent/mortgage $800

o   Water bill $30

o   Electric bill $60

o   Gas bill $60

o   Grocery bill $200

o   Insurance bill

- Life $25
- Health $250
- Fire $20
- Auto $200

- Foundation
  - Savings deposits of $100
  - Retirement investments of $250

- This would be a good example of monthly bills. They may fluctuate slightly; however, as humans, we are creatures of habit. Meaning if you take two showers a day, then your water bill will reflect that, and it is not smart to budget based on someone who only showers once per day. We do what we do consistently.

2. Liabilities

- Liabilities like bills usually cost you money monthly; however, unlike bills, they usually have a beginning and an ending date you will pay them till.

- Liabilities are money owed on items you are allowed to use or occupy as you pay them off. Another term for this is known as secured debt.

- Also, at the end of these monthly payments towards liabilities, you typically owned the object or thing you were paying.

- There are many examples of different liabilities, however, to name a few:
  - Car
  - House
  - Business
  - Land

- These are few examples of liabilities that you can finance for your day-to-day use such as.

    o   Furniture
    o   Equipment
    o   Appliances
    o   Cooking products
    o   Cleaning products

- Liabilities can be found in many forms, but a basic understanding of them are things you can finance to own.

- It is key to make sure that your liabilities, to the best of your ability, do not ever become greater than your income and your assets, except when the ROI is greater than the liability costs. We will get to that in the electrical wiring chapter.

3. Debt

- Yes. Debt and liabilities are two different things.

- Debt is something that you owe but usually does not benefit you. Instead, it usually benefits someone else.

- Debt is money borrowed that you owe and is not secured by anything. Also known as unsecured debt.

- There are several types of debt, but the type I like to go over is the first kind of debt which consists of you owing someone for them either giving you their money for your own personal use, business use, miscellaneous use or someone performing a service for you and expecting payment later.

There are many examples of this, some of which are:

    a.   Credit Cards
    b.   Loans
    c.   Line of credit
    d.   Medical debt
    e.   Auto Service Repairs debt
    f.   Borrowing from someone

Most of these are perceived as bad debt; however, there are ways this debt can also be good debt. For the purposes of this section, we are only going to focus on bad debt.

Bad debt is debt that you have from one or more of the examples listed above. That usually comes with a cost associated with repayment. This cost associated with repayment is typically called interest. It is wisest to pay off the debt with the highest interest because this will cost you the most money overtime. Many or all of these can come with interest; however, usually, credit cards and loans come with the highest interest. It is best to pay these off first, not that you neglect the other ones, only that it is okay to pay the minimums on those until your highest interest debt is paid off and then use your payments to go towards the lower interest debts.

Examples:

- Credit card A has a balance of $100 with an interest rate of 24.99% per month and a minimum monthly payment of $10.

- Credit card B has a balance of $300 with an interest rate of 15% per month and a minimum monthly payment of $25.
- ABC loan has a balance of $1,000 with an interest rate of 5% per year and a minimum monthly payment of $50.
- Bank A line of credit has a balance of $10,000 with an interest rate of 2% per year and a minimum monthly payment of $75.
- Elbow Feel Funny Hospital has a balance of $15,000 with an interest rate of 1% per year and a minimum monthly payment of $100.
- Your Car Works Fine Now Auto Company has a balance of $2,500, the same as cash, with a minimum monthly payment of $250.
- Borrowed $250 from a friend, the same as cash with no minimum payment.

It is important to approach your debts strategically and write them down before deciding to aggressively pay off a particular debt. As you see in this example above, it may be easy for you to decide which option is the best. If you only have a monthly budget of $600 between all the companies, it costs $510 per month if you only pay the minimum balances. However, where you dedicate that extra $90 in your budget is going to be key. Also, the time to which a particular debt is going to exist at the minimum balance is also going to play a key role in how you decide to pay off your debt.

Typically, most will tell you to put aside the borrowing from your friend since there is no interest nor is there a minimum balance; however, the person in this example (your friend) is the most important person. Having that relationship to help you in future endeavors is important; however, severing that relationship may be to your detriment in the future. Though this person is important, you still want to look at the two credit cards and the interest that they are going to accumulate monthly. By looking at this, you are going to see that you need to make a greater amount than the minimum for those credit card payments while still prioritizing your friend. Credit card A has an interest rate of 24.99%; therefore, you need to pay at least $25 towards it per month at a minimum upfront. Credit card B has an interest rate of 15%; however, the balance is $300. Therefore, if you only pay $15, you will lose $30 per month; therefore, at a minimum, you need to pay $45 towards credit card B. This puts your total outward spending on debt at $555. This means that with a budget of six hundred, you can afford to pay your friend $45 per month.

Though there is no interest on your friend's loan, it is important to maintain the relationship to make sure that your friend continues to trust you in future endeavors. At this rate, your friend will be paid off between 5 and 6 months; this eliminates one of your debts. You only have four more months to pay off Your Car Works Fine Now Auto Company. Continue paying off the auto company at its minimum since there is no interest that will be accrued at this time. During this for months, you still have $90 that you will want to put into credit card A. This will eliminate most of the balance except $10. This means that you can eliminate credit card A's debt next month and put $80 towards credit card B's debt. This will drop that balance to $170, and because credit card A's balance was settled, you now have $25 in addition to your $90, totaling $115, and only 2 more months to pay off your car repair. In these two months, the first month, you pay $115 towards credit card B, and in the second month, you only pay $55 with a remainder of $60 that you can use towards your ABC loan. In 10 months, you have now paid off the lender, Auto Company, and both your credit cards.

Your loan now only has a balance of $440, give or take the interest, your line of credit has a balance of only $9,250, and your hospital bill is down $1,000 with a balance of only 14,000.

This may seem intimidating at first; however, if you still just continue to pay the minimum balances on your line of credit and your hospital bill, in less than 2 months or a year, you will have paid off your loan completely and will have $500 to go towards your line of credit. At the end of the first year, you will have accomplished eliminating all except for your two largest debts with the least amount of interest accruing.

Consistency is key, but if you apply the $500 to your loan each month in the next year and a half, you will have paid off your line of credit and have a balance on your hospital debt of only $11,600.

With your budget of $600, you can have this paid off in 20 months, you will be done with all your debt.

All your debt would have been taken care of in approximately four years. These four years may seem like an eternity, but it is always going to pay off in the end so long as you continue to look at your budget and adjust your spending two invest and save rather than stuff and things with no known ROI.

Don't Nail Your Hand

If you only have a hammer in your toolbox, everything starts looking like a nail. Debt is that hammer. We use it for everything, from groceries and gas to utility bills and vacations. Debt is not the answer. We are constantly finding uses for the hammer (debt) in the most unnecessary circumstances. There is no reason to ever go into any form of unsecured debt. You may think medical bills are out of your control, but they aren't, that is what health insurance is for. You may have raised the deductible to save money, but if you follow the steps for building a solid foundation, your path will be straight regardless of the obstacle, no matter how great the challenge. Unsecured debt is not a tool for anything but sorrow and misery. Make it a point to pay off all your debts, especially unsecured ones. It is not worth the heartache of trying to dig yourself out of a hole repeatedly.

Often, people lie to themselves about the financial burden, and stress debt has over them. The only surface is the vacation trips, exclusive activities, and new fancy car. As an insurance agent, professionally, I can say that the stressful and undignified way these people speak to me is much different from the stories and photos they post on social media. Their lives are mostly a string of lies and deceit, while their true selves are shown to me over the phone or in person. You may be thinking, "they can afford it; they're earning millions as influencers." High Income and low net worth are still broke, living paycheck to paycheck.

I once had a customer who called my office 2-3 times weekly regarding her bill. She was so stressed, and her account constantly hovered above $0, occasionally dropping into the negative. She had a brand-new current-year expensive vehicle and a huge, expensive home with her husband. Their children were grown up and out of the house, so the couple lived in this magnificent home alone. This customer was always late on her bills, playing catch-up every month until one day, she forgot to call me to stop the automatic draft, and the account draft caught the bill up. She called in livid, saying I should have known to stop her bill and how I dropped the ball. She told me I needed to issue her a refund for her owed payment. At the time, I was new and inexperienced, so I told her I'd try to refund her. The company, of course, denied the request, and I had to break the news to her, and this infuriated her even more. At this point, I said, "well, ma'am, if you don't have the money to pay, you might not be able to afford us at this time," just trying to be helpful. She erupted, saying, "you blankety-blank, I make $91,000 a year, and my husband makes $110,000 a year, I make more money than you'll ever make; you don't know anything about me...," I interrupted her asking' "Then why can't you pay your bill on time?" The phone was silent, and then the call dropped. About an hour later, her husband called the office asking for me, and he was furious. When I answer, he doesn't even let me get through my spill before he lays into me. "You disrespected my wife, you don't deserve to work there, you had no right talking to my wife that way, etc.," Once he finished yelling at me, he asked what the problem was, to which I responded there was an overdue balance on the account that was just drafted out and his wife said that it put her in the negative. He was puzzled at first; then he asked how often this happened. I told him every month. He didn't say anything else to me, and the next thing I heard from him was, "[Wife]! What the..." and the phone disconnected. He called the next day, spoke to a co-worker of mine, and paid the entire annual payment in full; he was extremely upset because it turned out his wife was taking the money he gave her every month for bills to go shopping. Be careful of those who look as if they are "rolling in the dough" because they just may be "rolling in the debt."

This just goes to show living above your means is not just for low-income people, it is for everyone. You cannot out-earn an unstable financial foundation no more than you can over-build a structure to no longer need a foundation. Unsecure Debt is not an emergency fund, a backup plan, or capital for an investment. It is signing your life over to the ownership of the lender. You must work harder, seeing less of the fruits of your labor the greater it expands. $1,000 in the bank is greater than a $5,000 line of credit. Unsecure debt carries with it an array of undesirable effects: adverse incentives, false sense of security, overspending, underestimating, delayed freedom (as opposed to delayed gratification), and overcompensating, unsecure debt works against you on all sides.

Example:

This is the same person in two different scenarios. Sarah is a young adult that has been working for two years now. She is not the typical woman, she has few friends, and they have weird hobbies. They all have low-income jobs and enjoy eating out together and designing costumes for conventions they like to attend. These are not expensive hobbies, but little by little, they do add up over time. She will have two ways to resolve her monetary problems. One with debt and the other without.

Debt

Sarah wakes up and receives a call that her friends will be meeting at a local coffee shop this Saturday morning. Sarah, without a second thought, agrees to meet them. She arrives, and they are just chatting casually, talking about the good ole times. Sarah is asked by the barista what she will be having, she orders a large caramel macchiato with extra pumps of caramel and a pastry. Then since she arrived later than her friends and they had already finished their drinks, she offered to buy them another. They all decline except for greedy Cassie. She wants a large of what Sarah is having. Total bill: $15.00. The groups of friends continue to talk until one of them gets a text message about an early bird special for the next convention coming up. Usually, the tickets are $100 per person, but this special is only $75.00 for today. Everyone brought tickets immediately except for Riley, who could not afford her ticket because she was waiting on a paycheck next Friday. Sarah offers to buy her as well to make sure she can get her ticket too. Riley offers to pay Sarah back, but Sarah gets 5% back on all event purchases, so she tells Riley not to worry about

Cash

Sarah wakes and receives a call that her friends will be meeting at a local coffee shop this Saturday morning. Sarah, before deciding to go, looks at her checking account. She currently has $300 in this account and may have a bill or two that are due to draft, totaling around $100. This means she only has $200 to spend before her next paycheck this coming Friday. She decides to go out after looking into this. She arrives, and they are just chatting casually, talking about the good times. Sarah is asked by the barista what she will be having, she orders a medium caramel latte with extra wiped cream, which is free for $2.50. She notices that they have all finished their drinks, so she asks if they would like to come back to her place so she can make a meal for them. They all agreed to go back to her place but declined the food, all except greedy Cassie. Once they got back to Sarah's place, the groups of friends continued to talk until one of them got a text message about an early bird special for the next convention coming up. Usually, the tickets are $100 per person, but this special is just $75.00 for today only. Everyone brought tickets it. Sarah and her friends leave the coffee shop and decide to go to a few stores to see if they can buy materials for their costumes. Sarah gets on a spending streak making sure she gets all the right materials to make the best costume. She visited 5 different stores to find the best discounts on the materials. She saved $50 from the store sales and only spent $250, plus she had to get gas to fill up after driving around all day for $40. Sarah was happy with all the purchases she made that day because of the deals and the bonuses she received from the credit card. Though the convention is 3 months out, Sarah is happy she can prepare early.

Total Spent: $455

Credit Card offers 5% back on events, 3% back on Gas, and 2% on all other purchases. Sarah also saved $50 in deals and drove to the cheapest gas station she could find.

Total "Savings": Credit Card Bonus - $13.70 + Store Deals - $50 = $63.70

Sarah makes $15/hr., which means it would take over 30 hours to make the amount she spent back, plus the Credit Card interest rate is 22.70% APY or $8.61 every month on the current balance or 30 mins. of her time at work.

immediately except for Sarah and Riley, who could not afford their ticket because they each would get paid the next Friday. The convention wasn't for 3 months, so that was fine. (Both of them waiting out, and 2 weeks before the convention, someone sold them their tickets for $50 each because they couldn't make it) Sarah and her friends search for costume ideas online and place some items in their cart. Sarah decided to purchase two pieces of material every paycheck until the convention for $45, which she waited until receiving her next paycheck to start. She was able to design a beautiful costume in time for the convention. Sarah was also happy she got to hang out with her friends that day.

Total Spent (that day): $2.50

Total Spent (in general): Costume - $225 + Ticket - $50 + Coffee - $2.50 = $277.50

Total Savings: $455 − 277.50 = $177.50

Sarah was able to design a great costume for just 3 hours of her time each paycheck at work.

This is an example of how the same situation can be well organized and planned or adverse and stressful later. The two scenarios, though made up, are real in that they repeatedly play out in our society. Bad decision-making does not lead to good outcomes. They lead only to more bad decisions followed by destruction. Check your account before making purchases, not your credit limit. Making frivolous purchases should be a section of your budget, not a category for debt. There are many things you can do with your time and money, but the moment you use debt on your purchases, you become a slave to the lender.

<u>Types of Fasteners</u>

Screws are nice but not necessarily essential; however, if there is room in your budget, these things/stuff can keep you from slipping into depression, anger, hopelessness, and meaninglessness. Therefore, this section will focus on stuff and things.

1. Stuff

   • This is defined as the loose intricacies and trinkets on the inside of your home or transportation vehicle.

   • Stuff can be useful, entertaining, and detrimental as well. No matter what stuff you have, none is necessary; it is preferential.

   • There is never a case when you need stuff; stuff will never save you, nor will it help you financially;

however, it may benefit you outside of your financial goals.

- Stuff varies from cheap to valuable. The value of stuff usually determines its usefulness; however, these are not always correlating factors.

It is important to note that stuff is not a necessity because once you understand what is necessary, you can gauge how much stuff you can afford. That stuff is unnecessary, and it does not mean you cannot finance it. This you might confuse with debt; however, it is self-inflicted, and at the point in which stuff takes priority over your financial goals, the Everything Else in the foundation becomes heavy and unstable. This has the potential to destroy your financial foundation.

Example:

a. Josh is an aspiring DJ artist. To make the quality of music he would need to succeed, Josh would have to get a professional speaker, professional turntable, professional DJ mixer, and a high-tech desktop computer. This all is going to cost him about $6,000. Josh currently has $2,000 saved up, and the store is willing to let him finance the rest. Of course, if he makes good music, he may never have to work a day in his life; however, if he does not, he will spend the next 5 years paying for all the equipment that he started financing.

b. Sam wants to be a chef. To be a chef, Sam needs to purchase special kitchenware, including silverware, pots and pans, plates, gloves, etc. Sam goes to a kitchen store to purchase everything that he needs to get started, and after pricing everything out, it looks like it is all going to cost him about $2,500. Sam has the $2,500, but it would cost him everything that he has in savings and investments. If Sam does well in his cooking career, it would not matter how much he had to invest today, but if something goes wrong before then, he would not be able to get back on his feet for a while.

c. Jasmine is a dancer. She does it in her free time, usually after work. Jasmine must get some dancing equipment, and after looking at the dancewear, makeup, and costume, she will need to perform it comes up to $200. Jasmine has $5000 in investments, $2,000 in her savings account, and $500 in her regular checking account. She can purchase all the items she would need to start performing for-profit without having to touch her investment or savings account.

d. Tony likes to play video games. He plays them in his spare time to clear his mind from the hardships of the day. Tony's good at playing and may be able to go to a tournament. The winner of the tournament receives $100,000. To enter, Tony needs to purchase the most up-to-date Alienware Computer on the market today. This equipment cost is $5,000, there is a $50 entry fee, and he will have to take 5 days off work. Tony has $4,000 in Investments, $1,500 in his savings account, and $400 in his checking account. This tournament would cost Tony all but $400 of his savings and Investments. The days off from work could cost him his job (income for the week, and there is no guarantee that he would win.

There is nothing like having a dream and going after it, especially one that may one day produce an income. However, it is always important to look at the whole picture and recognize whether a particular purchase is a necessity or stuff. In the examples listed above, there are four different scenarios in which all have potential gains and losses; however, the deciding factor of what is a necessity and what is stuff, no matter who you are in these scenarios, is considered stuff for the potential career or hobby. Stuff is simply something that you purchase that is not needed for you to survive. This does not mean that it would not be of benefit to you, it just means it is not required to live. That aside, we are going to break down the wisest options for all the scenarios.

e. Josh would have to spend not only all his savings and Investments but also OPM. (Other

People's Money) this concept is often praised; however, it takes a seasoned investor to navigate these often-harsh waters. If Josh is as good as he believes he is and works diligently, he should take only a portion of his savings and get stuff as he can afford it with his own money. This will continue to build the character that Josh will need to sustain this dream. He should continue working and saving and buying little at a time because though he may never have to work again, the reality is using OPM could cost him more than it could gain. By buying products one at a time as he can fully afford them, he will build skills that come along with the new equipment as he can afford it.

f. Sam would have to spend every dime that he has. This may seem good to do because he has it to spend. However, always remember Murphy's Law. Apply the same reasoning Josh should use to Sam's situation, apply wisdom in purchases, and start a YouTube channel that generates an income to subsidize the expense of purchasing all the items that he will need. A good gauge of how well he does or will do may come from avenues such as YouTube. People are very honest on the internet, and this may prove to benefit Sam overall. This will give him a level of accountability that will follow him in his cooking career in the future and make him a better cook as opposed to looking the par and not having the skills to follow.

g. Jasmine's scenario is by far the best; however, the same rules apply to her; whether she spends $200 or $2,000, she should apply the same logic as Josh and Sam in the scenarios above. Though she is already a good dancer, refining her skills in front of an audience may prove to benefit her overall. She should get only items she needs to dance as opposed to the extras and continue to save and invest as opposed to dumping all her checking accounts into this career.

h. After gauging all the previous scenarios, Tony should fall in line; there are so many Avenues to becoming successful in gaming than just entering a single tournament. He should evaluate his success online and continue to save and invest and search for opportunities that he will be able to enter overtime as he develops his skills and continues to grow in the gaming world. It is not a bad idea to start a gaming channel as well.

Overall, stuff may or may not earn you income, it may only make you feel good. However, it is important to evaluate and recognize the stuff that is in your life and to ensure that your finances are not tied up in stuff.

2. Things
- A thing is something that takes up space, whether in your home, your car or in your stomach. It

takes up space, but it is not a necessity. This would be your curtains as opposed to just having blinds, it provides your home with decoration and adds atmosphere. Also, putting rims on your car may add Style to it. Lastly, going out to restaurants and ordering your favorite meal with dessert really makes your day, especially if you feel it is deserved after a long week of work. These things all have something in common, and they are just things. Things that do not contribute to your life outside of the connotations that they hold to you. There is nothing wrong with things, only the need to recognize that they are just that, a thing.

- Things have a place in your life; typically, they come after a budget is set in place and bills are taken care of.

- It is important to note that you should never go into debt over things. Adding an additional financial strain on your wallet is unnecessary. No matter how much you want a thing, whether it be food, an accessory or otherwise, it is not worth your financial freedom.

- There are some things that you can purchase that disguise themselves as a necessity; however, they are not; they are only a thing.

- **Example**:
  a. Your room already has an overhead light, but you do not like overhead lights, and therefore you feel

the need to purchase a lamp. The purchase of a lamp is not a problem; however, it is a thing. This thing can be replaced and should not be prioritized if the rest of your foundation is not set in order. Sometimes sacrifice is the best way to get ahead to make sure that your foundation is set in place.

b. Growing up, while you were with your family, you always had a TV in the living room. This was the largest TV in the house, and though you may only have a small TV now, you feel it is important to get a large TV for the living room. Understand that television is always going to be a thing, it will almost never enhance you as a person. If the television you decide to purchase is more than you can afford, do not purchase it, instead, save and come back when you are able to. Typically, there will be something better once you have the money to purchase the first one.

c. It is Friday night, and you are just getting off from work, you have had a rough week, and you feel that you should reward yourself with your favorite meal at your favorite restaurant. This may sound great on paper; however, you do not want to set yourself back with the purchase of a meal that will temporarily make you feel good for a moment but may have serious setbacks on your mental state and your finances as well. The act of eating after bad circumstances conditions your mind that when bad circumstances come about, rewards come after. This causes you to subconsciously produce negative circumstances in your life; therefore, you can reward yourself, which perpetuates a cycle of failure.

- As a rule of thumb, you should always save three times the value of an item (thing) that you want before purchasing it. This is called delayed gratification. The concept allows you to take a step back and evaluate as you are saving up three times the value; when you are finally ready to purchase the item that you want, you may find that it is marked down and or there may be a more advanced version of the thing that you wish to purchase in the same price bracket as the item that you wanted to purchase originally. This works for more than just things, and this also works for Stuff, liabilities, vacations, etc.

Pipes
Losses, Emergencies, Misfortune. Overspending, Under Budgeting, and Large Unnecessary Expenses.

Just as every living thing has waste, human beings have developed a plan that routes waste through pipes and an intricate network of sewers that lead to depositories that are then recycled and reused again, which is salvageable. "We are drinking the same water that the dinosaurs drink," my dad always said to me. Likewise, financially there is always waste that is produced. They come in various forms, and no matter how financially competent you are, waste is a byproduct of life. There are good types of waste and bad types of waste. Everyday we are thankful that plants give off the waste of oxygen so that we can breathe. Likewise, the waste that you give off fertilizes the ground; however, the waste that some large oil companies and construction companies produce is bad waste, not just for the environment but also for the world at large. This chapter will cover all types of financial waste, both good and bad, that most people encounter in life.

Many times, people try to eliminate waste altogether; they will set a goal and go for it full fledge. They will start or continue saving in more aggressive ways and with much more vigor than before. They will move in with family, stop going out with friends, never spend anything on themselves, etc. Depending on their personality and the timeframe of their goal, this is sometimes successful (for a little while). This plan is unsustainable and leads to a violent backlash of your mind rebelling against the neglect of your personal well-being. People are holistic in nature and while saving or growth may be a goal, remember the outlet (waste) must match the goal. If you want to be aggressive in your saving, you must also be aggressive in your rewards. Not necessarily dollar for dollar, but if you want to save $10,000 and you only make $50,000 per year, the 20% saving goal you have for whatever goal you have must include milestone rewards that are not counterproductive but rewarding to keep you on track towards your goals. I.e., a fun hobby you enjoy doing after a hard week's work, an activity you have never done before monthly, a mini vacation every quarter, or an extravagant restaurant experience every month. These may seem to undo your accomplishments, but quite the opposite, they enhance them. Imagine you are trying to eat healthy but do not allow yourself to use the restroom; though you are eating healthy, the backup bile in your body would be making you unhealthy and sick. This is the exact same thing that happens when you refuse to spend any of the fruits of your labor. You may mentally be fulfilled but slowly build up emotional bile that will backfire on your progress. You will be more prone to misfortune because your emotional state has a lot to do with your outlook and your outlook has a lot to do with your outcomes in life. If your savings account is growing, but your personal life is declining, you become irritable and angry, in that anger, you may speed while driving and or drive recklessly in general, which in turn leads to you getting pulled over by the police or worse, getting into an accident. Both will have dire financial consequences putting you back right where you started to begin with. Do not allow yourself to get "stopped up" with emotional bile, conversely, do not spend so much of your time building emotional fulfillment that you neglect mental waste either, both are detrimental.

In short, there is a plumbing plan and network that works together to make your pipes run smoothly and not cause a backup. This chapter will go over the piping problems and help you produce a plan that allows you to combat the bad waste and maneuver the good waste necessary for success.

<u>Plumbing system for the disposal of waste.</u>

Where there are good habits, well-intentioned, and well thought out plans, there is misfortune and just plain bad luck. Of course, not everything that happens to you that is bad is your fault; however, the most important thing is to take ownership of the newly developed problem in your life. Putting off problems or excusing problems because something that happened to you was not your fault only disables you. Taking ownership of the problem enables you to find Solutions and fix it.

1.   Losses
   •   Where there are gains, there are losses. These losses may happen in the market, they may happen in a side

business that you may be venturing in, or they may come about in wage cuts at your job. But, no matter the cause of loss, damages can always be mitigated.

- For starters, insurance, especially in that of Property and Casualty as it pertains to property and personal items and life and health as it pertains to health wellness and death.

    a.   Property insurance protects your personal and real property from losses that may occur under the circumstances specified in a particular policy. This means that certain losses that come about, such as theft, fire, and even weather is covered under certain circumstances minus your deductible. A deductible is what is deducted from the total amount of damage assessed that is covered by the insurance company.

Example:

You get into a car accident that is your fault, and you have a deductible on your car of $1,000. The damage to your car is $5,000; you will receive a check to either you or the car repair company for $4,000. You will be responsible for having $1000 to go towards the damages to your vehicle. (Remember, 78% of the country does not have $1,000 in case of an emergency. If you are one of them, please lower your deductible to what you actually have in your account)

b.   Casualty Insurance is the liability portion of the insurance policy. This pays the amount that the other party may sue you. In the example listed above, the damage to the other party may be more or less than the damage to your own vehicle, in which case the insurance company will pay for the damages to the other vehicle as well to protect you from this loss at no additional charge to you unless you are sued above the limits that you hold.

c.   Health insurance protects you against injury, sickness, disability, rehabilitation, and general check-up losses that occur in your lifetime or your dependents. Some health policies do so much as to extend paying for loss of wages over a set period. Such policies are typically extremely inexpensive and usually range from as low as $3 to $20, depending on the amount of the payout, your current health, and your age.

d.   Unlike the name, life insurance does not mean it pays for you to live or because you have a hard life. That is not exactly the loss that life insurance covers. Life insurance is coverage for you or someone you have a financial interest into payout if you or a loved one dies. This may seem morbid; however, it is not for you to necessarily be in a better state due to the loss of a loved one or yourself. Life insurance is to protect you against the financial burden that is associated with death. If a parent were to pass away and you still lived with them sometimes, they leave debt, outstanding bills, dependents, and of course, their funeral cost behind for you or a loved one to manage. Life insurance is undervalued, yet everyone needs it. There is no guarantee that you will use any other insurance except life insurance; we will all die someday. WILL, not MIGHT!

Example: Jessica is 18 years old and deciding which college she would like to attend. She has some good scholarships, but none are a full ride, including room and board. Her mom can give her a few thousand dollars; however, her health is declining, and her medical bills are piling up; despite having health insurance, the amount that they are willing to cover still leaves her with a large amount. Her mom tells her that she has life insurance of $100,000. The following day Jessica's mother passes away. Currently, her mother's medical bills are $15,000, she has a mortgage with $30,000 left, and Jessica needs $25,000 to live on campus, and the typical funeral cost is anywhere from $8,000 to $12,000. If we average out the funeral cost to only $10,000, this leaves Jessica, the sole beneficiary of the policy, $20,000 left over after all expenses are paid for. She will need this for day-to-day expenses that her mom would have been able to pay for had she been alive. The $100,000 policy in this case, would be able to pay for all of Jessica's new expenses now; however, this is not always the case. In more than a few cases, children are left with new expenses, and their parents either do not have life insurance or do not have enough life insurance to cover the expenses their child will incur. This is not always just the case from parent to child; sometimes, it is from Child to parent. Oftentimes we believe the younger you are, the less of a chance you have of dying. Though this is true in most cases from natural causes, it is not always the case from accidental death and unexpected illnesses. Because it is less probable that you will pass away at an early age, life insurance is less expensive while you are young; however, it is often not purchased because of the assumption that nothing will happen to a child. The cost of funerals does not change, they are still $8,000 to $12,000, and funeral homes are not in the business of giving away free caskets and free services. As cruel as this may sound, it is best to just be prepared for such losses.

• Losses are not always in the form of items in which you can touch. Some losses are intangible, such as in the stock market. In addition, losses may be final or temporary. An example of a final loss would be if you invested in one company (i.e., a single stock) and that company goes out of business, you have suffered a loss that is irreconcilable. However, an example of a temporary loss is one in which you invested in a mutual fund as an example. Not that mutual funds do not suffer final losses; it is just a lot less likely. Since mutual funds are a compilation of many different companies or stocks that make up the entirety of the whole, one company going out of business will not affect the overall stability of your investment. So, if one company goes out of business out of a hundred companies, you may suffer a temporary loss, but if you continue to keep your money in the mutual fund, typically, it will continue to go up, as history has shown us.

- The last type of loss for practical purposes is the loss of wages due to the loss of a job. This is the type of loss that typically stifles growth. While harmful, if one is not prepared for such losses but with an adequate foundation, this should only be temporary. There may be certain governmental provisions for such losses, such as unemployment benefits and food stamps; however, these should not be used as a crutch; rather, they should be used to lessen the loss until work is found. If your foundation is complete and your 6 months of savings is in your savings account, and at least 9 months was in your investment account, not including what may have accumulated in interest, also your life insurance may have accumulated cash value by this time as a last resort you may be able to borrow against the cash value and in some cases withdraw dividends without paying them back. This is the foundation, and if all of these arc maintained, you should ideally have up to 1¼ years of job-searching before you tap into any loans from your life insurance or dividends or even unemployment or food stamps. However, utilize the tools that are around you, so if Uncle Sam allows you to use said benefits, you should be free and able to do so without even having to tap into your savings and Investments or life insurance until you are able to get yourself a new job or create a business.

2. Emergencies

- First, let us define what an emergency is. An emergency is something that comes between you and food/water, shelter, and health. Transportation is not an emergency, not looking well according to your standards is not an emergency, not having furniture is not an emergency, not having a lot of space is not an emergency, not having internet service in your home is not an emergency, not having a cell phone is not an emergency, not having hair products is not an emergency, not having things that make you comfortable is not an emergency, having bad credit is not an emergency and lastly not having cable TV is not an emergency.

     - This may sound contrary to everything that you have heard in the past about an emergency. If your car breaks down on your way to work and you're unable to make it to that job, and that potentially puts you at risk of losing that job, first understand that unless your car breaks down and puts you in direct harm or direct danger of being in harm, there should be some things in place that can get you going. The 6-month savings is for emergencies, yes if you lose that job, it will impede on your food/water, shelter, and health; however, your insurance should be able to, at a minimum, tow your vehicle and at any given time. You should have in your checking account enough to mitigate certain things such as car repairs or have small joint savings account with a 1% savings drip from your income for small things such as this as well. If you live on public transportation, you may just have to rearrange your traveling schedule to make it to work. In any case, transportation should not be a reason to tap into your savings account. Purchase something that you can fully afford repairs and all associated expenses (i.e., taxes, insurance, and gas), and keep maintenance on your transportation to ensure certain things, preventable things are no recurring issues. Emergencies do arise if you are to lose your job due to your vehicle breaking down or some other reason. Whether in your control or out of your control, most losses you should be able to mitigate. However, there are a few unpreventable losses that require you to tap into your savings.

      a.   Health can be a very abrupt emergency that needs to be addressed immediately. With certain coverage in insurance, this emergency should be eliminated with only minor amounts to you, depending on the severity of the illness. Addressing such issues sooner rather than later saves you overall. Health is a reason, if necessary, to tap into your savings account.

b. Food/Water is the most pressing issue, if unable to get either of these, you must tap into your savings. Anything that impedes your food and water is a necessity. As shown in losses, there are certain governmental assistants such as food stamps and WIC that are there to help with certain expenses such as these in times of emergency.

c. Shelter, whether mortgage, rent, or taxes, is a huge reason to go into your savings. Remember the rule of three, 3 minutes without air, 3 hours without shelter, and 3 days without water, 3 weeks without food. This is a rule of thumb as it pertains to an emergency. Without shelter, we are nothing. If the rent is not paid, it only takes up to 30 days for an eviction process to start. For a mortgage, it is only about three months, and for taxes, it is only about a year

before your property is sold, and you may be
forced to leave your home.

3. Misfortune
- These are the woes of life, all the things that
emergencies were not in the emergency section. These are
just simple things that go wrong. As creatures of habit, we
simply do things that may or may not benefit us, but they
are merely habit. In doing this, we tend to overlook things
that we do, such as everything. More often than not, we do
the math for only one or two aspects of a particular thing we
want. This goes back to the example of the car in the
foundation section oftentimes in the beginning. If we do not
have three times the amount to purchase a particular vehicle,
it may not be worth it. The reason is simple: more than just
the payments of the car or the car itself are the problem in
the equation.

Example: If a car costs $10,000 and you only have
$10,000 and buy it in cash, you have forgotten vital
details of this car purchase. Depending on your age and
driving record, and in a lot of cases, your credit,
whether you finance the car or not, plays a factor in the
auto insurance. If you have spent a hundred percent of
what you have on just the car, you will not be able to
register the car because the taxes on the car can be
upwards of $1000 to $2,000. The taxes are not always

this high, but in impulsively purchasing a vehicle for the exact amount that you have saved, you have miscalculated an important detail in the purchase. Therefore, you have forgotten the down payment on your auto insurance; whether you choose to pay it for the entire year, semi-annually, quarterly, or monthly you will not have it this month. Also, it may be customary that vehicles have a full tank of gas when you purchase them; however, this is not a given, and therefore, this also needs to be equated. Lastly, it is also not a given unless you purchase a brand-new car that the maintenance on it will be up to par. Therefore, this is another factor that needs to be included in the purchase of just a measly car. At the end of the day, there may be upwards of an added $10,000 that will need to go into this $10,000 car that you would not have been prepared for on the basis that you only saved up exactly what you needed to purchase the physical item.

• Many misfortunes come about from simply not doing the math due to habit. Yes, misfortunes happen outside of your own fault; however, taking ownership and responsibility for your own life is important to ensure that misfortunes do not break you. Some key things to keep in place are not to prevent misfortune but to mitigate the damages that misfortune brings.

a.   First, once you have reached your foundation goals, you should start a Drip Savings Plan in addition to your current savings. This is a plan in which you will add to your 10% savings each month an additional 1% or a flat dollar amount from your paychecks. Regardless of which method you choose, it is advisable to open a joint savings account in the same financial institution for quick access and transfers or build your checking account by the base of the 1% or flat dollar amount per month.

Example: If you earn $4,000 per paycheck and put away 10%, you will save $400 per paycheck; however, once you have reached your foundational saving goal of 3 to 6 months' worth of savings of $4,000 to $8,000, then you open a savings account at the same financial institution as your checking account and deposit 1% of your income or a flat dollar amount like $50 per check. This would be $40 per paycheck at 1%.

This method allows you to continue growing in excess instead of simply waiting for an emergency to happen, then watching your savings diminish all at once.

b.   Though misfortune is unforeseen and sometimes unpreventable, oftentimes, regular maintenance on your car(s), appliances, and other mechanical, electrical, and regular-use devices will prevent the inevitable. Maintenance also comes in the form of advice as well. Regular maintenance includes talking to your boss if you have one, a teacher in class to prevent the financial risk of failing a course and having to retake it, a banker, tax accountant, or financial advisor for financial insight and understanding of certain obstacles that he or she can guide you around. This is one maintenance that most people miss; thus, they are unaware of the pitfalls in the economy, interest rate spikes, bull or bear markets, tax advantages, exemptions, risk management, and regular relocation of your assets. This maintenance is one of the most important but undermined until tragedy strikes. Lastly, health maintenance, annual doctor visits, semiannual dental cleaning and bodily detoxing, quarterly cholesterol, blood pressure, and weight checks, monthly workout assessment (i.e., max out weight training, personal best record on running, swimming, and aerobic workout) and daily workouts and multivitamins. This can prevent most health problems, promote healthy brain function, and prevent fatigue, allowing for the most productivity and preventing most avoidable health-related expenses.

    c.   Having health insurance is self-explanatory; however, there are many more insurance products than most people are aware of. There are also warranties and scheduled item insurance which is 100% coverage on any item, e.g., jewelry or electronics coverage if they are broken, lost, or stolen. Insurance protects your real and Personal Property once a loss has occurred. Insurance is not usually preventative; however, some companies will help with maintenance or discount rates due to upkeep maintenance. Insurance also protects against death and health expenses which are typically the heftiest expenses anyone will encounter. The coverage usually starts with health insurance which covers most medical bills. Sometimes this leads to death; however, this is not the norm, depending on the circumstances. Albeit death is a certain eventuality, we will all face it one day. Though the people who pass on, obviously have no expenses, the loved ones they leave behind always do. These expenses range from burying the loved one to bills they left behind (e.g., medical bills, their portion of the living expenses, and debt). Life insurance can and usually does covers all these expenses and more. Sometimes it works to pave the path for the wealth development of the dependents they left behind.

d.   Do the math! The most encompassing aspect of avoiding misfortune is arithmetic. Start with adding all expenses in a month, then adding all your exposures (i.e., Home, car, home appliances, valuables, and dependents). Next, add up all the liquid money you have saved for

expenses, assess the disparities, and plan accordingly to
fill in these disparities with insurance and warranties,
then reassess your 3 to 6 months saving fund
accordingly.

Example: Approach your finances like a word problem to
find the various disparities.

Monthly expenses: $2,500

Total amount of exposures: Home ($250,000), Personal
Property ($20,000), Car ($10,000), Home Appliances ($5,000),
Valuables ($3,000) and Dependents 2($1,500/month) =
$289,500

Total Liquid Saving: $10,000 or 4 months of saving.

Total in Investments: $15,000, not including interest

Disparity: $274,500

Knowing these numbers is essential for insurance and
warranty amounts needed.

Homeowners Insurance: $166/mo.

Renters Insurance: $15/mo.

Car Insurance: $100/mo.

Home Warranty: $60/mo.

Personal Articles Policy (Valuables): $5/mo.

Life Insurance (Dependents): $50/mo.

Hospital Income Policy (Dependents): $15/mo.

Disability Income Policy (Dependents): $10/mo.

Total: $421/mo.

Using the information given, you may not be able to afford
all this insurance protection at once; however, you can now

adjust your $2,500 monthly expense to $2,921 and save accordingly for insurance if you still meet your 3 - 6 month saving goal. Three months of this new expense would be $8,763, which means with your $10,000 savings, you can maintain it. Though this may seem like a huge increase, this is much easier than saving the $274,500, and 100% of that money is always at risk. In addition to this, the legal protection that you would need to have always and would also be provided with insurance, as opposed to you just hoping for the best and planning for the worst.

4. Overspending

•   Overspending is the antithesis of compound interest in that once it starts, it continues to increase and compound. Compound interest is the process of money growth over time, like a snowball going downhill. The more time, the more the increase. (i.e., Five percent interest on $100 is $5, whereas, on $100,000, it is $5,000.) Overspending always starts off small, like one splurge meal on the weekend, even though you have food at home. It will only set you back $10, no big deal, right? Not exactly, most fast food loads their meals down with sugar and preservatives, which are more addictive than crack and nicotine. This makes you less likely to go home and cook because you want more of the addicting food that clouds thoughts and impairs judgment. Before you realize it, you are back at your favorite restaurant again and now making excuses as to why you need new clothes right now. Once you look up, it is two days from your paycheck, and you are flat broke with nothing to eat, "guess it's time to fast and pray." Overspending is a character and discipline problem, not an income problem. More income will not stop this problem; it only makes the purchases more expensive. This is known as the "Diderot Effect," which I will explain in greater detail later in this chapter.

- The solution to this problem is observation. Looking at your account rather than budgeting is a more direct approach to this problem. Where if you create a budget, anything within that budget is a free game, if you budget $100 for clothes shopping, you will spend close to or all the budgeted amount; however, if you watch your account, you can spot negative trends early and stop spending sooner. This creates discipline and builds character.

5. Under Budgeting

- As discussed above, budgeting is not the most viable solution to overspending; however, it is important as it pertains to bills and income. Bills and Income are, for the most part, consistent, but there are times when they fluctuate. Being aware of said fluctuations are key to financial growth.

Example: Income is $3,000/ month, and your usual Expenses are $2,000 leaving a $1,000 gap with which you can splurge. Though this is the norm, and you typically spend this $1,000 on things you want, i.e., clothes, restaurants, and other things, this month, the gas bill went up $200 because of the winter weather. If you spend the money that was due for this bill without looking at it because it was out of the norm, you have catching up to do, and if this is multiple bills at once, it hurts even more.

- The solution is to look at your bills and your income to ensure that nothing has drastically changed because companies do not care about your lack of planning, nor do they wait on your response when a bill has changed. They simply send out notices and draft the amount that is due to them. Do not underpredict what is due or under budget in this regard. It will hurt in the end.

6. Large Unnecessary Expenses.
- Large unnecessary expenses are the ones you lie to yourself about to conflate wants as needs when you have a large, unexpected surplus of funds. Like stuff or things, this problem is either perpetual or massive. (i.e., purchasing a $4,000 stereo system for your car, purchasing a patio set without maintaining the patio or ever spending time outside in the first place for $2,000, or taking an unanticipated and unplanned vacation for $5,000) These large, unexpected expenses are not bad in and of themselves they are just unnecessary at the time. The simple remedy for this problem

is a budget and designate times for expenditures. It is quite common to have these sorts of expenses when large sums of money come in, and they are unanticipated.

- There is a difference between large unnecessary expenses and large anticipated expenses.

Example: Paying for a paint job or a stereo system when your check engine light is on for $3,000 because you just made $3,500 due to a refund check or a bonus at work would be considered a large unnecessary expense. Whereas evaluating first what the problem was with the check engine light allocating the funds towards this problem, and then using what is left on either painting or adding a stereo system would be a large anticipated expense. Finding out to fix the problem would be $1,000, then spending no more than $1,000 on either a paint job or a stereo system.

- Proactivity is a great deterrent to large, unexpected expenses. Plan for what to do with all funds, whether large or small, but especially unanticipated large surpluses or funds to be allocated towards things that earn you money or towards large anticipated expenses. Being proactive in the arena of large unanticipated expenses is a written plan that eliminates impulse beforehand. Do not depend on your willpower because it will fail you. Typically, it does not start off as one or multiple large expenses; usually, it is your first expenditure that determines the remainder of the large surplus or funds. For this reason, it is important that your first move is to always save 10% of any funds or income received, with no exceptions. Though eating out at a restaurant seems enticing, this leads to compound spending.

● Compound spending is the reverse of compound interest. Whereas compound interest is the accumulation of funds invested over time, leading to growth via the interest in addition to your contribution. Compound spending is the tendency to spend more once you start spending on something unnecessary towards other unnecessary expenses by impulse. This is also referred to as The Diderot Effect - The tendency for one purchase to lead to another. This tendency leads to financial ruin by compounding small and large alike unnecessary expenses that are unnoticed due to the lack of preparation.

Conduits
Income, Cash Flow, Dividends, and ROI

The passage by which energy travels throughout the entire structure, powering it with the ability to harness electricity without the immediate aftermath of fire. These are the pathways that transfer energy, converting it to light, a/c, cooking, storage, heat, and other electronics. This may seem basic if raised in a developed country, but this concept is still out of reach for many people around the world. Its significance should never lose its savor to you whether you see it as luxury or an everyday convenience, it is power, and with all power, as most know, the famous line "With great power comes great responsibility" ~Ben Parker from the movie *Spiderman.* *

This concept is important as this chapter goes into the terms that can create or are creating great power-generating wealth tools that, for most, are unused and for some, only heard of but not utilized or not utilized correctly. To the untrained eye, these four terms are the same thing, but they are quite different to those who can tell them apart. Light can be created in several ways, and to some, fire may be the best or the only way you know how to create light, other people know about the fire but have also learned to catch fireflies and other illuminating naturally occurring items, but only a few use a light bulb. If asked which works the best, most, if not all, would say the light bulb; however, only a few know how to make it. Finances are predicated on what you know. Learning is the key to financial liberation, and application is the art of understanding.

Electricity powers the entire structure

Conduits run through every portion of the structure to generate power. Income is the conduit by which your financial life gains power. This is within every part of your life because it determines or should determine your financial decisions. Your income determines how much you can spend, the total amount your budget cannot exceed, and your financial proclivity. This acts as a ceiling that cannot be surpassed within a month, quarter, or year; however, if not abound by it, will lead to an imbalance of finances, thus producing debt and anxiety.

1. Income

- Income is generated in various ways, falling into two categories: active and passive. Active income is any income that you work for, exchanging time for money. Passive income is the act of exchanging money for money. Unfortunately, the money you work for, exchanging your time for is taxed the highest. Still, it has the largest benefit as this opens the possibilities for greater passive income opportunities.

    a. Active Income is earned income, and therefore, it has the most weight to it in several ways. This means it has the most effort dedicated to it and the most time and energy. Because of this time and effort, it is important to have all cylinders firing to make the most of it; getting the most out of your work is key to the success you will have, both at the workplace and at home in most cases. Active income is not always just the money you earn from work, it is also the affection and attention you receive from your family to pour into them. As holistic beings, people who balance their time with family, spiritual growth, personal entertainment, self-improvement, recreation, and work perform better in each of these areas because they do not allow these separate sections of their lives to blend. You will find your life overwhelming when you allow these areas to bleed into each other.

    b.   Passive income is unearned income that uses the resources and savings you have obtained towards investments that yield returns. Whether it is equities (stocks), partial ownership in shares of a company, rental income from a property or properties you own, high cash value life insurance, high-interest savings, or other "safe" minimal risk investments, passive income is money spent that makes you more money. The term "spent" is important to note here. Understanding two major principles here will better equip you in the future as it pertains to how you allocate your money.

    i.   The first principle is that everyone spends 100% of their money every month. How? We all allocate the funds in the following ways: bills, stuff & things, travel (i.e., gas, Uber, Lyft, maintenance), groceries, bank account(s), savings account(s), brokerage account(s), retirement account(s), insurance, rent/mortgage, or cash you keep. You may be asking yourself how is putting into an account and for that matter keeping cash "spending money" isn't that the definition of saving it? In theory, yes, but you are spending it on a bank or financial institution's services that are insured by the government, and so long if it stays under a certain amount and the country as we know it stays in existence, at least longer than you are alive then your "purchase" was worth it. If not, then what you spent your money on was not worth it… should have spent it on a Swiss Bank Account. (Not really) The concept remains the same, though; you spent it and are happy with your purchase unless you were around during the Great Depression when accounts were not insured, you have gone unscathed. What about the money you keep in cash? How is that money spent? This is money spent on inflation and depreciation. Now you might say, "well, that's not fair," but the reality is indecision is a decision in and of itself, and just because you decided to keep the cold hard cash does not mean it is not being spent every day. Remember, every month you are spending your money, even if it is going into a savings account, and you will have the proof of time letting you know if that was a good decision or not in the future. Therefore, it is important that you make the best decision available to you at the time, which will be discussed shortly in this section.

ii.   The second principle is that risks are in every investment, there is no such thing as a 100% safe investment, and you must decide the level of your risk tolerance. This rule of thumb helps you in several ways, namely, re-evaluating the word safe. This is important because whether you are prudent or risky, loss can occur to anyone at any time, and it is important to note that your stewardship of funds should include a portion of your investments in something a little riskier than your threshold to expand your comfort level, to allow you to grow. Growth is an essential element to investing because the ability to grow expands your (the investor's) ability to yield returns. If you sow a little seed, you WILL reap a little harvest; however, if you sow abundantly, you MIGHT reap abundantly. This is where you must decide if you would rather invest a little and gain a little or trust yourself enough to make a sound investment that will yield you the best returns your current ability can yield you.

Example:

- If you put $5 into a money market account at 2%, it will yield you $1 in **10 YEARS!**

- If you put $5,000 into that same account, it will yield you $1 every **3.65 days**
- If that financial institution went out of business, you would be insured by the principle only and the interest gained, not future value. Given this information, if the financial institution closed 6 months after you opened the account in the first example, you will have only gained half a penny. However, in the second example, you will have gained $50. There is, however, a case where the interest was not insured and you will not have gained anything. The point remains that if you sow sparingly, you will also reap sparingly regardless of the amount of interest or the lack thereof, you can only get out from what you put in. The "might" aspect is because there are no guarantees of return, only good chances and risky odds. This goes for everything; whether you are referring to the principal amount, the interest, or the initial investment when it is a low return or investment, it can only at best, yield low returns. This principle prevents many would-be millionaires from coming into existence due to extreme financial conservatism.

- Income is where maximization is key to having the greatest outcome in your financial future. Again, maximizing increases your income by strategically working hard, working smart, and working efficiently. Seizing opportunities at your job for overtime, making additional sales goals for yourself to increase commission, growing, and developing a realistic plan to move up in your company or start a side business that grows into a full-time self-employment career. Be proactive in your employment, and never reactive. Start the day early and plan what key things need to be accomplished for your day to be maximized to the fullest potential. Make a to-do list of no more than three important tasks that need to be done for your job to be successful. This is strategic planning that allows you to reach your fullest potential on a consistent basis.

- Income is the outcome of the time or money put into a particular opportunity. Whether a job, career (yes, it is different than a J.O.B. as discussed previously), investment, real estate rental, interest bearing account, life insurance cash value, business, or hobby for pay, income is always an opportunity. It is important to remember that it is and should not be taken for granted. 2020 should be a lesson for all people; whether you increased or decreased financially, the reality is there is not a person that does not know someone that lost some or all their income. Income is the way by which your money is made.

2. Cash flow
- Cash flow is the way in which your money moves through your household or business and is usually determined by your dexterity and your ability to manage operations and household expenses, growth, and debt.

• If income is the power line leading to the grid to which all the power to your home is predicated, cash flow is the electrical lines that run through your home that power the individual outlets and switches. This is the process by which all your money is given a name. Outlet, if you will. This process must be written and habitually followed. The reason most people fail is because they depend on their own willpower. Willpower is a horrible plan for success; though most people think that willpower is all that they need to succeed, the people that are the most successful are on autopilot most of the time and do not rely on willpower unless necessary. Success in your cash flow is to follow the outlay of the plan of where your lines will run each month without thought.

• In the first section of the book, the foundation is laid, as discussed, no one thinks about the foundation once it is laid. So are the foundations of your finances. If you have already determined that 10% of your income is going to savings, 15% is going to be invested, and 10% is going to tithes and offerings, and then you have decided on autopilot that you will live off 75% of your income. This means your bills, activities, meals, and travel expenses will come out of 75% of your income. This 75% is commonly referred to as operating expenses (OPEX). The easiest way to make sure no thought goes into this decision is to have these percentages automatically go to the accounts with the designations if your job allows you to. This allows you to be responsible with little effort or thought.

•   Regardless of income, the amount is useless if your money is not going to the right places. Keep in mind power is supplied to the house, but if a wire is severed, no energy will flow. Money flows through your household as electricity flows through to the various outlets; however, if a breaker is off or for some reason, the flow of electricity is blocked in any way, this causes problems. How you resolve these problems determines your future success and finance. Some believe that power is the problem and therefore focus all their energy on getting more power (income). You can get five jobs, two side businesses, and rent out a room in your home; it will never be enough. Oftentimes income is not a problem; it is cash flow. When you do not have enough money to last the rest of your month, you panic, get upset at yourself and make rash decisions. One of which is to go into debt, this is the equivalent of instead of hiring an electrician to come out and fix the electrical problem, you try to patch this up yourself and hoping your power lasts and a fire does not ignite.

•   Debt is that patchwork. It very rarely is the solution to any problem as it pertains to cash flow. There are instances where debt is required to reach certain goals; however, they are calculated risks, not whimsical ones. Debt is not meant to be long-term, consumer debt, that is. Obviously, mortgages, lines of credit, and other long-term secure debts are exceptions to this rule, but a credit card should not be a go-to in monthly expenses. This leads to ruin quickly. There are two main debt types: consumer debt and secure long-term debt. Consumer debt is unnecessary and can often be resolved by time, which is waiting to get what you want instead of just going out and getting it. Secure long-term debt is one that cannot be reasonably waited for to obtain over a short span of time, such as a year or two. This is a calculated risk that allows you to get or make a large purchase while also reaping the benefits of that purchase's value (I.e., house, business, or land) and is also known as secured debt, as we discussed previously.

Example:

- Consumer debt
- Charles has a job that pays $50,000 a year, this breaks down to $3,400 a month after taxes and health insurance. Charles does not participate in his company's 401K plan to save any portion of his income. Charles also has a misunderstanding of his total income; he has merely divided $50,000 by twelve and is expecting $4,166.66; therefore, he subconsciously spends over $700 more than his actual income every month. Charles has bills of $3,000 a month which includes gas and groceries. However, Charles does not know this information. Every month, he spends $300+ on restaurants with his girlfriend and another $300 or $400 on activities and dates, putting him in the negative by over $300. He subsidizes his habits with credit card debt. He

always says that he never spends more than what he has and therefore pays off his credit card bill at the beginning of every month; however, he is in a constant cycle of debt that hinges on his employment which he is completely unprepared to lose should something happen. 3 months later, Charles does in fact, lose his job. He has $0 in retirement and $0 in savings with a $3,000 credit limit, and $400 of it is spent. Charles, however, does not panic; he figures he has about 3 months to look for a job. He has his last check, which is only $1,700, and he still has $2,600 worth of credit which is only $4,300. With Charles's overhead of $3,000 per month, he only has a month and a half before he truly needs to get employment offering the same amount of income. Shortly after losing his job, unbeknownst to him, his health insurance cancels as well. Just a few weeks after he becomes unemployed, he has an incredible pain in his right leg and is forced to go to the hospital without insurance. It was determined he had a pinched nerve, and it was due to stress and anxiety. Without health insurance, his bill came out to $2,000 just to be seen, and if he were to do an operation, it would come out to over $10,000. Charles, now devastated, because he knows what the problem is but does not have the income or savings to take care of it, leaves and drives himself home. Because he had this pinched nerve problem, his foot locked down on the gas pedal, and he could not move it, running through a red light and getting t-boned by a truck. They sent him back to the hospital with a broken arm, cracked ribs, fractured femur, and a concussion leaving him unconscious. Though this was due to a health condition, the accident was deemed to be his fault which significantly reduced the amount of coverage he would receive. Charles believed that "full coverage" on his vehicle meant his injuries and his hospital bills were covered. Charles did not realize that "full coverage" only includes liability, comprehensive, and collision insurance which only pays for his vehicle and the other driver's injuries and their vehicle. It does not cover medical payments unless you have this coverage as suggested by his insurance agent, which most people do not have. It also does not cover disability, permanent or temporary, due to his injuries which is included in some plans; however, it is mostly not included or talked about. Full coverage is assumed to be something that it is not. It merely translates to the state mandate and loan mandates that only covers the vehicle, not you. Charles's injuries were well over $40,000, and with no health insurance and not enough auto insurance, Charles may be out of work for at least 6 months to heal or must choose a lower-paying job where he does not have to use his legs. Charles is not in a good place right now. He is now over $40,000 in debt and physically broken. Once again, Charles is faced with two choices, just as everyone else is, when trouble arises due to the inevitable:

o   Blame life (i.e., boss for firing him, insurance guy for not telling him, parents for not educating him enough on life, or the world for not being fair to him), or he can take responsibility for lack of planning. Though you cannot prepare for everything, not preparing for anything is a plan to fail everything.

o   Take responsibility, acknowledging himself as the procuring cause of everything that has happened thus far, his lack of planning and his fast-paced lifestyle as the reason for his failure. This will give him control, whereas blaming external forces, though it feels good, takes away his control. If he blames even one of the forces, how can he change his life, the person and or thing would have to change it for him; therefore, his freedom, peace of mind, and control are in their hands. However, if he is the one who got himself into this situation, he alone can pull out of it. It will not feel good for him at the time, but this way, he can make real steps to get out of his current situation and into the place he needs to be.

•   This entire situation services as an example of unpreparedness and responsibility. The responsibility falls on Charles in this scenario anyway. Whether he chooses to accept it or not, his life will never improve until he does. If he decides to blame the world for his problems, even if the world came back and said sorry to him, there would be no steps for him to take to get out of his current situation. However, if he does take responsibility, whether the world comes back to say sorry or not, he would have already moved on.

Example:
- Secure long-term debt
- Katherine purchased a home in an up-and-coming neighborhood around the new construction of businesses in the area. She did some research, and though today the property started with low value, she looked at the trends of the market and saw that there was potential in the future. She purchased her home using a secure long-term loan (mortgage) and waited for 5 years in a home that she liked but in an area not yet developed. In those 5 years, she updated her home several times with appliances and updates that would increase the value of her home. By the end of these 5 years, her home had increased inequity of $50,000. She then used that $50,000 as a down payment for her new home with a mortgage payment of $1,200 and rented out the property that she used to own for $1,700 a month. After paying her new mortgage, she is still able to clear $500 worth of profit per month. This allows her to grow her income by using unearned income or passive income to subsidize her lifestyle. The key to secure long-term debt is forethought and delayed gratification. There must be a plan before any action is taken, and there must be steps that lead up to the desired result. Katherine not only delayed her gratification for the first property she lived in, but she also

matched her job's 401k plan as well as insured the assets that she had, including herself. Katherine managed to save up a small nest egg of $40,000 in 5 years as she was living in the home. She, too had rainy days, but her rainy days were covered by either her savings, her insurance, or by her willingness to wait out the storm. (Time) This was only the start of Katherine's story but more on that later.

3. Dividends

• Dividends are regular payments of profit made to investors who own a portion of a company, also referred to as a stock. Another type of dividend is also a return of premium on life insurance policies that, if a mutual company, will be paid to their policyholders and are also not taxable; however, that is a topic for another book.

• Dividends are the difference makers of all energy in your structure. This is like energy-efficient upgrades to your home, power-saving light bulbs, efficient HVAC system, and high energy efficient rated appliances. Dividends act as a drip of saving from good investments. They are seamlessly running in the background to further your financial gains and increase to the point of compounding. This principle, though enticing, is a waiting game but rewarding once understood.

• Dividends are merely a paycheck on a large investment you have made. The return made can be reinvested or taken. This is particularly important because many people do not give it the time or the amount to grow to its fullest potential. This goes back to the example in the passive income section of not being able to reap abundantly if you sow sparingly. To compare this to your current job, if you have a job where you are not required to have a high school diploma, college degree, limited mental skills, extensive labor, general skillset, and hourly (no results based), you have an easily replaceable job and are usually paid the least. However, on the converse, if you have a job that requires an MBA, multiple licenses, specific skills, a lot of mental capacity, and results-based outcomes, this is usually a high-paying job. This is because sowing time and money in abundance reap the rewards in abundance at your vocational occupation. It costs for you to go to college, learn a trade/skill, get a license, read books, and practice; therefore, the more of it you do, the better you are paid for it in the workforce. This is because you intrinsically gain value the more knowledge and or skills you get. If you think of yourself as an investment, the more you put into yourself, the more you can gain in dividends paid out in the form of a paycheck. Dividends work the same way. If you purchase a stock and never invest in it again, meaning you only own one stock on that company's best day, gaining the highest percentage it is ever gained, you will only get a fraction of the growth at a 4% dividend rate. Whereas if you owned 2,000 shares of that stock at a 4% dividend rate, you would have gained an annual wage. Not all investment shares pay dividends; however the ones that do, you would be wise to put a generous percentage of your investments into these for the maximum benefit. These stocks are typically referred to as Blue Chip stocks. Some mutual funds also pay dividends as well, but the vast majority are individual stocks which can be risky; however, Blue-Chip stocks show the most stability and are typically sure investments.

• Dividends are dispersed in several ways, most notably is reinvested and paid out. The difference between the two makes all the difference in the overall investment and how it will perform overtime.

o Reinvest dividends is when the dividend payment is put back towards the principal investment. This is the equivalent of an additional payment towards your overall portfolio.

Example:

• Jorge invests $100 monthly into a blue-chip stock, and the company pays a 4% dividend every quarter. The market is bearish, which means it is going down, but Jorge continues to invest. Each stock usually costs $150 per share; however, the stocks are now $100 per share due to the market. In 3 months or one quarter, Jorge purchased three stocks at $100 per share and he chose to reinvest his dividend of 4% of the overall amount he invested. This means that his dividend payment of $12 will be automatically reinvested. The $12 buys a partial stock of .12 at the current price. This reinvested dividend does not appear to be much; however, overtime, this small portion continues to grow, and in 5 years, Jorge has invested $6,000. He continues to invest as the market continues to fluctuate. Of the $6,000 he invested during this time, his dividends would have doubled his investment to $12,020.45, and this only expands the longer Jorge continues to invest. With the market increasing back to its original $150 per share, Jorge's $100 only buys two-thirds of a share, but it produces a larger dividend. At this point, his dividend is now a considerable income while he invests. This is considering that the stock grew back to $150 a share, which, divided over 5 years, is 9% growth per year on average, and the dividends purchasing more stocks as well has a higher return than if it were just interest alone. That would have only grown his $6,000 investment to $7,627.15 in five years. Albeit, either option is better than if he just put $100 into a savings account with no interest equaling only $6,000 over the same period.

4. Return on Investment (ROI)
- ROI is the amount profited from an investment after all costs. The simple formula for this is: ROI = (Gain from Investment - Cost of Investment) / Cost of Investment. This is a straightforward way to gauge that the money and/or time you spend doing something is ultimately worth it. Making assessments in a situation prior to a final decision should go through the filter of ROI.

- ITR is a quicker version of this to decipher whether a decision is profitable to you or not. ITR = Investment, Time & Return, which is a much quicker way to decide whether something is worth your time or money.
- Using these two methods are great tools to eliminate the bottleneck of the day and ensure that you make the best decisions with the options, information, and resources available to you at the time.

Financial Direction

Blueprint
S.M.A.R.T. Goals, a Budget, a Plan, and the End in Mind. <
Self & Spouse / Family

Schematics
Recap, Put it all Together, and Make Good Financial Habits. <
Self & Spouse / Family

Gathering Materials
Giving & Tithes. < **Self & Spouse / Family**

Blueprint
S.M.A.R.T. Goals, a Budget, a Plan, and the End in Mind.

Forethought. There is much to be said about forethought, yet here it is at the end of this book. Why would forethought be the last thing to focus on? Shouldn't thinking come before actions and all financial decisions, namely, in this book? Forethought should be the first thing to focus on rather than the last thing. However, human behavior is predictable, habitual, and lazy, meaning the brain relies on "good enough" rather than highly efficient. Nail biting rather than budgeting, smoking rather than planning, eating out and overeating rather than dieting, social media as opposed to spreadsheets, etc. The brain has no intention of making you successful financially or otherwise, it only seeks quick fixes and immediate gratification. Forethought has no place in the brain's primary, secondary, or tertiary functions, which is why all success starts first with building a habit of success, learning along the way, and making the path that inevitably leads to freedom. "Ready, Fire, Aim!"* This is the way to success, doing what you know to be right and learning why it is right along the way. Saving 10% of your money is not easy to do. Investing 15% of your money is not easy to do. Opening a college fund account for a child that you have or for future children is not easy to do. Buying a home, having your first child, opening a business, and whatever you may associate with success is not easy to do.

However, with the right habits, mindset, and a plan, not the best plan or even the longest detailed plan, but a plan will make these hurdles doable. Do not spend your wheels trying to make the perfect plan or the best budget, or even read all the greatest books of all time, just start. Have an end in mind, and go for it. In his book, The Total Money Makeover, Dave Ramsey says that winning with money is 80% habit and 20% knowledge*. This is true, and you must start today. When you get your paycheck, do not even consider it; take out a calculator, then enter the number on your paycheck, multiply it times 0.1 and put that amount in your savings immediately! Put your paycheck amount in your calculator again, multiply it by 0.15 and invest it! In what?! Well, not in a fancy coat, a down payment on a car, or a new blender. Put it into a designated broker account which most banks they have, and if not, Fidelity Bank and Vanguard are two options to invest. If you are truly unsure about any of that, put it into your company's 401k or IRA. Don't think, do!

My wife and I started a rule of thumb in our household that you may find helpful for investing. If it is good enough for us to use the company's products or services, then it is also good enough for us to invest in. We used our spreadsheet as a guide for what to invest in. (e.g., Verizon Wireless VZ, Planet Fitness PLNT, Apple AAPL, Google GOOGL, Comcast CMCSA). We would pay the bills for the service and then invest in the same company as well. Been doing this since 2017 and it has worked out well. It is also a good indicator of when you should leave a company's patronage as well. If the stock is in a nosedive and you are consistently losing, stop investing in the company and switch service providers. We believe we should support and benefit from the companies we use regularly. I am neither a financial adviser nor my wife, but if it works, it works.

The Apollo 11 was off course 97% of the time on its way to the moon, yet they still reached their destination. Having the perfect plan means you miss all the time it would have taken you to get there. Start with the end in mind having very pointed goals, such as aiming for the Moon and charting your course. You will make mistakes, but in the words of Thomas J. Watson, founder of IBM, "Would you like me to give you a formula for success? It is quite simple, really. Double your rate of failure." To put that simply, do not be afraid to make mistakes; in fact, make many mistakes, but learn from all of them. How long will you sit there and think about which company might be the best to invest in rather than just invest in it and see for yourself? This may seem rash and even a bit unsettling but ask yourself, "what do you truly have to lose at 15 cents on the dollar?" The difference between the most successful person in the world and you right now are that they were not afraid to fall because they knew they would get back up stronger every time, and instead of making every happy hour like your uncle who "almost made it", they actually did. Choose to succeed, and no failure will stand in your way.

Nevertheless, a plan is still required. Without a plan, there is no direction or plan of action, which leads to misery and ruin.

There are many who protest budgets, diets, itineraries, schedules, and any form of forethought planning of any kind as they feel they limit freedom and the ability to choose. However, it is quite the opposite, these methods free up more units of time and energy throughout your life.

Example 1:

Going on a vacation is one of the most freeing experiences. However, when it is a couple going on a vacation, there is often one party that wants an itinerary and schedule and the other that wants absolute autonomy and freedom. Which party wins is a complete toss-up, but if it is the autonomy and freedom party, you are in for an unfulfilling, often lazy, lounging around, and sometimes miserable trip which is why most people get back to work stating they need a vacation from their vacation. This usually is a trip of one or two outside excursions of drinking, eating out at restaurants, one club or event, and the rest of the time lounging in bed and watching TV. It is extremely unrelaxing and unfulfilling. The alternative, however, itineraries and schedules factor in all the rest time that you need while packing your vacation full of activities that bring you closer together and are extremely fulfilling. As previously stated above, nothing goes 100% as planned, but the forethought makes for an incredible adventure when plans are changed in the heat of the moment. A major restaurant is closed, or a tour gets canceled, but now you arc on a different side of town where you can have new experiences in the time you allotted for that excursion. Finding a new experience in the same area or at a different restaurant makes for lasting memories and a fulfilling vacation. Just a plan, not perfection, is better than no plan at all.

Example 2:

At the beginning of the month, a couple desperately needs a budget. One of them wants to put it together and do it before the month starts, and the other feels constricted and restrained and does not want to have a budget because it will put them in a box. Therefore, no budget is made, and when the month starts, they are frugal and shop sparingly. However, once they get their paycheck, they start to spend very rapidly, without thought. This led to the collapse of their finances and an argument that almost ended their marriage, complete with yelling, throwing, and ultimatum statements such as "if you don't..." or "I am never..." This almost led to the collapse of their relationship, simply a lack of planning and forethought. Spontaneity in your finances for all items is not freeing at all but constricting. The following month the couple, after having that enormous fight, decides to input a budget. In doing so, they listed a few items that were important to both of them, prior to the month beginning:

        ○   Recurring bills (including saving, retirement, insurance, real estate, and investing)
The Foundation

        ○   Gas for vehicle

        ○   Groceries for home

        ○   Toiletries and personal maintenance (i.e., hair, nails, makeup, etc.)

        ○   Car maintenance

        ○   Home maintenance

        ○   Eating out at restaurants

        ○   Vacation fund

        ○   Fun spending

With all the items that they wanted to accomplish in an average month listed and followed, they were able to accomplish a lot more with a lot more freedom to do things that they wanted to do without worrying about their finances. This created more time for intimacy between the two and virtually no arguments as it pertains to finance.

Example 3:

High Schoolers are given an assignment to write out their 5-, 10-, and 25-year goals. This assignment was supposed to be fun and enlightening to show what the goals were that each student set out for their lives. However, most of the class did not take this assignment seriously and instead took it as an opportunity to collaborate with one another and speak on things that they would rather do besides what they are currently doing. About 80% of the class blew this assignment off, whereas only 20% filled it in. Of the one hundred students that were assigned this, only twenty of them wrote descriptive and realistic goals for each of these year's benchmarks. 10 years have passed since this assignment was given, and only one student of the 80% has gone on to have a career in a completely different direction than they ever thought, but it was a high-paying position, nonetheless. The other seventy-nine students went on to work at dead-end jobs and still lived with their parents, hoping their thirties would be better than their twenties. With no plan or goals to achieve that is very unlikely. The 20%, however, had a 100% success rate in finding high-income careers though not all fulfilled, the correlation to their fulfillment in career varied based on how descriptive they were in their goal setting at the time. Every person in the 20% nearly doubled the income of those in the 80%, and the top 2% or two students went on to earn ten times the income of even the others in the 20%. The intentionality behind these students far exceeded that of the 80%. The 2% of all the students had laser focus and now experience more freedom than any other person in the class and the highest earning person in the class or the 1% earns more than 1.5x the other students in the 2%.

This has everything to do with intentionality and focus. Most people believe that this is luck or just a few are chosen for greatness, but if anything can be taken from this example, regardless of how lofty the goals were, and even if they were not fully met, the simple act of trying made all the difference. When observing those that are affluent and successful, do not write them off as lucky or chosen but ask them how they did it, implement some if not all of what they say, and do not envy them but emulate them.

Make A Plan

Freedom does not exist in chaos; only tyranny does. The day tells you what to do instead of you telling the daily life has no agenda, it keeps coming, and with no plan, you will fail. Though you cannot plan for everything, if you do not make a plan for anything, you will fail at everything. A plan is the building block of everyday, every day is the building block of every week, every week is the building block of every month, every month is the building block of every year, and every year is the building block of your entire life. No unit of time is too small to be taken for granted. The smaller the unit of time you focus on, the more successful you will become because of the numerous opportunities you have planned to succeed. *
Always remember that falling down is a part of the process; it is not the product of failure but a necessity for you to succeed.

The start of a plan is a thought into an accomplishment, destination, or achievement you would like to hit coupled with a time limit to this goal. Once you have a reasonable time limit to hit a said goal, break this down into yearly chunks, then monthly achievements, weekly measurements, and daily must-wins. This allows you to see the daily, weekly, monthly, and yearly progress towards your goal; however, the most elite, they break it down into hours, minutes, and even seconds; remember, the smaller the unit, the more successful.

Success, like anything, is a choice. It is a choice to be or not to be; regardless of your choice or the lack thereof, success is in the balance. Failure, on the other hand, is the default, you do not have to try to fail; it happens organically. Where there is energy applied, there is order, and chaos occurs when there is no energy. In nature, this is like a jungle with vines and plants chaotically competing for sunlight. The plants are out of control because no active energy is applied in the jungle; however, when you see a bird's nest, know that energy is required to make this. The nest represents order, and this is the start of what it takes to be successful. Every seed of success starts out as just a nest. If you stay at it will grow, just one stick at a time, a few leaves, blood, sweat, and tears and you will create the order needed to succeed. Making a plan is more than necessary; it is obligatory to make everything that you wish to accomplish work. A plan is great, but action is greater, and your plan must be one with the flow of your own life, moving in the direction you are going and like a river constantly in flux and changing. Your plan must be moldable to the realities of life constantly moving and ever-changing.

Most projects do not start without a plan. But even in the simplest of plans, there will always be complications. These complications are found in real-life applications or implementation of a plan which is why plans should not be overthought. There are three main components of a plan:

1. Start with the end in mind (Goal)
2. Take steps towards the goals (Action)
3. Fill in the gaps, recalibrate, and plan (Details)

These steps are in accordance with Ready, Shoot, Aim, which is the breakdown of all plans that work. Locate your target, shoot at your target, then calibrate where you are off. You will fail if you do these out of order, such as starting with the details without any life experience or a goal in mind. If you just go right into the action without a goal, you will be moving aimlessly and find yourself in an abyss of what will feel like perpetual failure. This section will review the breakdown of a good plan and how to implement it into your life in real-time.

The Infamous "One Day"

There is a topic that needs to be discussed before moving any further. "One Day, I am going to…" or "One Day, we will be…," these statements are stated frivolously everyday by individuals around the world. This statement might seem harmless, but it is not harmless at all, it is extremely counter-productive and overwhelming over time. "One Day" is not what I mean when I say Ready, Shoot, Aim. Saying one day you will do something different that you are not currently doing or you will achieve something you are not taking steps towards puts an overbearing amount of stress and expectation on your life. This statement inadvertently adds an item to your mental to-do list in life, diverging your attention from what truly matters to something arbitrary. This may not seem harmful, but it is. If you are one with high aspirations for life, like starting a business, owning an apartment complex, or becoming a millionaire, these goals require pointed effort and attention to accomplish. Adding, "One Day, I will travel the world," though not a bad idea, will cause this item to be put on the table, splitting your attention from your true goal to a side quest. Given enough of these "One Day" wishes and your carrying capacity is full. Carrying capacity is the number of items humans can focus on at one time. That number is 7 plus or minus 1*, but for optimal results, 3 items are recommended for the greatest results. Putting this information into prospective, how many "one day do you have out there floating around in your head? Nine, ten, twenty-three? Regardless of the amount, write them down and complete a handful at a time or scratch the impractical ones off the list. Focus is important when trying to reach one's goals; the fewer the items on the list, the more focus you gain.

The Infamous "One Day" is also harmful because of our intrinsic nature to self-sabotage when we are over-extended. Self-sabotage is common amongst all people; there are various reasons why, but the top reasons are burnout, over-extending, over-committing, and people-pleasing. Notice a trend?

Anytime we go over our carrying capacity, we lose our ability to focus, which causes us to destroy all the work we started. The stress and anxiety of not hitting your goals always catches up to you, even if they were never truly your goals at all. Our brains are so powerful that if you say you will or even want something, it will start a dual-processor in the way of creating that thing. This is a great tool when used correctly towards your goals but terrible when working duplicitously. Commit today to never say "One Day. Goals are means to be set in order, not all at once and with that being said, let's talk about goals.

Goals
There are several ways to format goals. Goals can be made traditionally simple using just the time method or long-term goals; 5-, 10-, & 25-year goals which are just a snapshot of where you would like to be in life at specific times or what you would like to have accomplished. Another method is creating S.M.A.R.T. goals that are more shortsighted to accomplish key objectives over the course of a year. They can be longer, but smart goals are usually ineffective when they go past an annual period. The acronym S.M.A.R.T. stands for specific, measurable, attainable, relevant, and time-based goals. There are a few other methods; however, the last one as it pertains to this book, is a budget. A budget is typically only a month long and allows you to measure progress, gain accountability, and accomplish key objectives throughout the month without stress

or much recalibration. Time-management daily schedule is
another goal-setting method that allows you to manage the time
in the day by writing out key objectives before the day begins,
usually by noon of the prior day. This is commonly referred to
as "Must-Wins," and the maximum must-wins should not
exceed three in a day. * By doing this, you can measure your
day-to-day progress and how it relates to your overall goals
without overwhelming yourself with a list of tasks by which
you only complete the unimportant busy work. Based on all
four methods, you may see that all can be applied at the same
time without one getting in the way of the other, and that is the
point. When you create the time method of goal setting, you
are setting the trajectory of your life. You will not have all the
steps at your fingertips of how to get there, but by doing this,
you will at least know where you plan to go. This should be set
first, then yearly S.M.A.R.T. goals, a monthly budget, and
lastly, daily must-wins. This might seem backwards, but it
absolutely is not. Why would you have a daily schedule or
daily objectives with no monthly plan, create a budget if you
have no goal for the year, and why would you create a
S.M.A.R.T. goal if you do not know where you want to be in
the future? This does not make sense intuitively, but if you ask
any child what they want to be when they grow up, very few
will say well; first, I need to make a schedule and accomplish
daily objectives, create a budget, then I need to create an
objective every year, and once I've done all of that I'll know
what I want to be in the next 5 years, then 10 years, and finally

25 years from today. That would throw anyone off if a child said that, because you would instantly recognize that as backwards thinking. This is the same as not having your goals in place after creating a budget. You may follow the budget for a few months, even a year, but once you have realized that you have nothing that you are aiming for, you will quickly jettison the plan and go back to old habits. This is the reason you must start with the end in mind; hence this section is called creating a blueprint. No architect ever started counting how many screws, nails, and supplies he needed before drawing out what he wanted his final project to look like. On the contrary, he first drew what he wanted the end to look like then worked backwards to create it. This is the same with your life; decide where you want to be and who you want to be, then work backwards to create that goal.

Long term goals

Many people start writing these down in the order of the years to come; they write down their five years, then their 10 years, and lastly, they are 25 years goals. However, this should be done in the opposite direction; first, ask yourself where you want to be overall, this may be 25 years, 30 years, or even 50 years, but this speaks to what you want the finished product of your life to look like. The things you want to have accomplished and who you want or see yourself being. Then drop down to the mid goals of 10-years. This is what is the midway point of your life or, in some cases, depending on how old you are, this may be the beginning of your adult life. This speaks to where you want the halfway point of who you want to be as a whole and where you want to be on the way. Finally, you should create your five-year goals. These goals should be your most aggressive goals because they set you up for the remainder of the goals you have for the rest of your life. If you do not tackle your five-year goals, then you will lose your momentum and, in some cases, the hope you have for the rest of your life. Truly put extreme emphasis on your five-year goals, not focusing on the quantity of goals but the quality of those goals.

25-year goals - The way you approach these goals is by thinking as big as possible. In business, this is referred to as your BHAG*, which stands for your Big Hairy Audacious Goal. This is the goal that deals with an immense amount of wealth, a strong term relational commitment (marriage, spiritual, familial), what you want to be known for, the places you want to have seen, and the accomplishments of your career and in life. This goal needs to be big and bold, with very few compromises. If you are married, this goal should be made together, sit down with your spouse, and decide who you want to be as a couple and where you both want to end up. If you are not married and thinking about getting married to the person you are with, you should ask each other about their long-term goals for the next 25 years and wait for an answer. Do not suggest anything, and in most cases, it helps to have the other person write it down so that each of your goals does not interfere with or persuade the others. This is the limitless goal that allows you to shoot for the stars with no refrain. By evaluating the goals of the two of you, you can better decide if you should continue a relationship together. It may seem harsh to cut off a person over goals, but it is better to do so early than to endure the heartbreak later after time and energy is invested into a relationship where there is not a meeting of the minds to begin with. Also, starting with the end in mind helps better create your path in the lesser time goals. When you decide what you want your life to be anchor in, it is easier to make decisions on the subsequent goals that lead to your ultimate goals.

Example:
- 25-year goal
  - Relational
    - Married
    - Two children
    - Five close friends
    - Host every Christmas dinner with all members on both sides of the family
    - Consistent prayer life praying at least every day
  - Vocational
    - Earning six figures in career
    - CEO or top-ranking officer in a corporation
    - At least five streams of income

- Work a career that you would work for free (fulfilling)
- Have a career where you can reach at least 25% of the population
- Educational
  - Earn an MBA
  - Become six sigma Black belt
  - Read fifty-two books per year
  - Have written thirty books
  - Be an influencer with a million followers
- Health / Wellness
  - Have less than 10% body fat
  - Have no preventable diseases
  - Be at peak fitness
  - Maintain libido
  - Have muscle definition with six-pack abdominal muscles
- Financial
  - Have a net worth of five million in liquid assets with ten million in all assets
  - Have enough passive income to never have to work again
  - Give a million dollars to a charity
  - Have no debt
  - Have money saved for my children's children
- Fun
  - Travel to all six continents

- Have taken a 6-month vacation to travel
- Done five things on your bucket list
- Invented something useful
- Be known by many

10-year goals - The way to look at these goals is to think in terms of your 25-year goals that are far less restrictive and unrefined. 10-year goals are a visual check mark to gauge where you want your life to be directed. These goals are the best-case scenario for the future you envision for yourself. Be open-minded with your 10-year goals, still direct, but with the highest caliber of the pointed goals you have for yourself. Focus on only the points of most importance, not that the other things in life are not important; they just are not as important as your main vision for your future. When putting these goals together, be brief and to the point, not over analyzing or being too descriptive. Make sure you are still using your imagination of greatness while being grounded all the same in the reality that 10 years pass by in a blink of an eye. This sets your sights right on target and guides your decision-making when you evaluate where you want to be. Goals are like a map, meaningless without a visual. Using a map does not help you without landmarks or a visual of where you are.

Imagine you can meet yourself from the future, time machines were just invented, and you get into one. It is who you meet, the person you want to be in the next 10 years. If the answer is no, why not? How can you get to that person, and who is that person? How is his smile? How is her skin, what is her outlook on life, and how did it get there? What hardships did they have to overcome? What paradigm shifts did they have to make? Are you prepared to make that reality come true? How have you prepared yourself mentally, physically, spiritually, and economically? The future is now, and the question is, are you ready? If not, how do you get ready for it now? Set a goal and stick to it. Once the goal is set, you manage your life to reach that goal.

Example:
- 10-year goals
  - Relational
    - Meet that special person that you want to spend the rest of your life with
    - Join a church
  - Vocational
    - Be the team lead in my company or manager
    - Have a small business or side business
    - Purchased at least one rental property
  - Educational

- Be enrolled in graduate school
- Read forty pages a night
- Published the first five books
- Have an established blog or vlog with 50,000 followers
○ Health / Wellness
  - Go to the gym everyday
  - Be able to lift 300 lb. on the bench press
  - Run 4 days a week
○ Financial
  - Have a net worth of a million dollars in total net worth
  - Have two passive streams of income that pay all bills
  - Give $50,000 to charity
  - Have a half a million-dollar home almost paid off
○ Fun
  - Go on three vacations a year
  - Complete two things on your bucket list
  - Have a design patent for an invention

5-year goals – This is the halfway point for the 10-year goals. These goals are most detailed and geared towards habit-building skills. These goals should be looked at as an exponential function rather than a straight line. That means at the end of 5 years; this should act as a catalyst for the 10-years rather than an exact midpoint. This is the same as building the infrastructure for the rest of your life rather than having hit all your goals. Remember, the deeper your foundation, the higher you can build. If you wrote these goals at 16 for where you should be by 21, you might be discouraged if you set unrealistic expectations for where you want to be if you do not have the proper foundation expectations. For instance, if you want to be a millionaire by 21 but you have no product, service, or idea of how you will make it. Realistically, this may be a 10-year goal, and your 5-year goal should be to find the business or method to become a millionaire. This is not to say that you do not need to have high goals, but *a goal without a plan is just a wish.* * You cannot wish yourself anywhere in life, you can only plan your way to where you want to go. 5-years is the foundational building blocks you need to hit your 10- and 25-year goals in the future. The reason this is an exponential function is because it will appear that no progress is being made while you pour your cement down.

Example:
- 5-year goals
  - Relational
    - Date someone or people with the purpose of asking meaningful questions for compatibility
    - Build a consistent prayer life
  - Vocational

- Intern or work in fields that you want to or see yourself in long-term
- Start saving and investing for startup businesses and rental property investment
  - Educational
    - Obtain first degree
    - Read twelve books per year
    - Complete a book writing course
  - Health / Wellness
    - Get a gym membership and go at least twice a week
    - Take vitamins daily
    - Walk three miles three times a week
  - Financial
    - Get a Financial Advisor
    - Obtain the tools necessary to start making passive income
    - Give to a charity monthly
    - Own your first home
  - Fun
    - Travel out of the country
    - Find a need to fill for an invention

Short-term goals

Short-term goals are goals set for a year or less. These goals are detailed and descriptive, with actionable steps rather than just concepts or ideas. The smaller the time, the more focused the goals are. Anyone can say something they want or even write it down, but the difference between those that reach their goals and those that don't are two things, looking at your goals regularly, even when you are falling short of them, and execution. A Harvard MBA conducted a study in 1979 regarding goals setting. Before graduation, the study concluded that 84% of the graduating class had no goals, 13% of the class had goals, but no plans to achieve their goals, and only 3% of the class had both goals and plans to achieve them. 10 years later, 13% of the class with goals but no plans were earning on average, twice as much as 84% of the class with no goals. However, the 3% with goals and plans were earning on average ten times the amount of the other 97% of the overall class. * This is a reality across the country; there are approximately 10 million millionaires in the country as of this writing, in a country of over 330 million. Have you done the math yet? That is 3% of the country, 82% of which are first-generation millionaires, which means jettison the myth that all wealth is passed down. It is not, it is goal setting and plan execution that makes the difference. This is so important because if you can get this, you can accomplish anything. Long-term goals are just that, goals or targets for you to aim at, but short-term goals are actual plans of execution. Though setting goals are good, the best you can hope for is to keep up with the Joneses, but when you master and plan execution, you become unstoppable. There are annual goals that you should make year by year, and these are S.M.A.R.T. Goals. S.M.A.R.T. Goals are an acronym for specific, measurable, attainable, relevant, and time-based goals which translate to a realistic goal that you can aim for in an allotted timeframe. You must ask yourself questions about your goals and why you have them. If your 10-year goals is to be the CEO of a Fortune 500 company, why would this year's smart goal be to finish binge-watching 5 of your favorite shows? Not that there is anything wrong with watching TV shows or streaming service programs, but it should not be a goal if it does not align with your true goals. You may watch here or there but understand it should not be a priority. S.M.A.R.T. Goals should be followed by a monthly budget. This section will show you how if you have never made a budget. A budget is what comes in and what goes out. It is as simple as that. You plan what goes out just as you do in the moment, only now you are fully aware of your spending habits rather than coming up short and never knowing why. Finally, a daily schedule to keep you on track with a keen sense of focus and urgency. The daily schedule reminds you of what is important, no matter what may be happening around you. Daily schedules also ground you and guide the lens by which all your decisions should be made. These three modes of planning are not the only planning tools out there. There are a myriad of planning tools, and I encourage you to find the method that works for you; however, within a year, you should have more than one. (i.e., annual, quarterly, monthly, bi-weekly, weekly, daily, hourly, and by the minute) Regardless of the method, the outcome should all be the same, planning and execution.

Example:

- S.M.A.R.T. (specific, measurable, attainable, relevant, and time-based) Goals
  - Relational
    - Write a description of the perfect partner/spouse/relationship with God (Specific)
    - Find no more than three people that could fit that description and favors your relationship goals with God (Measurable)
    - Go to a group or organization regularly monthly, weekly, and daily (Attainable)
    - Join a group that will lead you to the perfect person and relationship with God (Relevant)
    - Deduce the three potentials down to one by the end of the year (Time-based)

  - Vocational
    - Write a description of the perfect career/job/business (Specific)
    - Call and/or apply for three opportunities that line up with these goals per week or read and/or research business opportunities for an hour every day (Measurable)
    - Intern or volunteer at different companies or businesses that you see yourself potentially working at (Attainable)

■   Go to different organization platforms and webinars or info sessions that share insight into different fields and read books on topics in fields you are interested in (Relevant)

■   Do not allow volunteer or internships to go beyond a month if you do not see the opportunity as a career and choose a career or business by the end of the year (Time-based)

o   Educational

■   Research a field of study to get a degree in, purchase three books on these topics, and pursue a topic which you are most familiar with writing (Specific)

■   Study for each class for 2 hours per day, read nine pages per day, and write a paragraph per day (Measurable)

■   Complete three courses in college, trade school, and/or licensing course, read fifteen books in self-improvement, and write your first book (Attainable)

■   Take college courses in business management, take online courses on social media and influencing marketing, licensing courses in a field of business expertise (i.e., insurance, real estate, investments, etc.), and read one field of study content at a time (Relevant)

■   Complete a full college year in credits, obtain at least one license, read 1-2 books per month, and start a blog to get and maintain at least 1,000 followers by the end of the year(Time-based)

o   Health/Wellness
- Target three major members of the body, arms, core, and legs (Specific)
- Increase strength and endurance by 50% and take daily vitamins everyday (Measurable)
- Be able to bench press 200 lbs., squat 250 lbs., and do seventy-five sit-ups without stopping by the end of the year (Attainable)
- Join a gym and go three times a week and do daily short workouts everyday (Relevant)
- Increase strength and endurance by 4.2% each month to reach 50% by the end of the year (Time-based)

o   Financial
- Obtain a home loan for your first home with low interest, 15-year term, affordable (meaning you are not at your spending capacity), and allows you to live in a good area (Specific)
- Reach out to five loan officers per month to find the best terms (Measurable)
- Be pre-approved within 3 months of searching with your required terms (Attainable)
- Purchase two books and read local articles about the communities you are considering living in (Relevant)

- ■ Purchase your first home by the end of the year (Time-based)

  o Fun
  - ■ Look for a need in your own personal life and draw out or write a description of what specific thing would make your life easier in that respect. Be specific of what the helpful items should do (Specific)
  - ■ Write an outline of the components of the invention every day until complete (Measurable)
  - ■ Reach out to different departments to patent your idea every month you have a greater description to make sure you can get the patent (Attainable)
  - ■ Read two books on making an invention and obtaining a patent (Relevant)
  - ■ Have your first patent complete and process by the end of year (Time-based)

Make a Budget - This is the biggest curse word in most households. This is bigger than the f-bomb, bigger than politics, bigger than your child calling you by your first name, this is the dreaded budget. (What you cannot do) No one wants to be restricted and no one wants to be told what to do. Though this is the way most people think of a budget, that is not what a budget is at all. In a typical month, your paycheck comes in, some bills come out, and you spend the rest on habitual things. Whether it is food in restaurants, clothes, experiences, or otherwise, it is a regular recurring expenditure of money that eats through the rest of your money that somehow leaves you at $0 or too little money to do anything else in any other department. You say to yourself, "Next month I'll..." or "Why don't I ever have any money?" the truth is you will not change because habits are based on quick or short-term pleasures, not delay or long-term gratification. Mixing the two to gain long-term success with short-term pleasures is important. A better way to do this is to have Budget Parties or Budget Dates with your significant other or spouse instead of having budget meetings. If you are single, treat yourself to an enjoyable pleasure such as your favorite restaurant, watch your favorite movie, or play a game with the numbers. The purpose of this is to stimulate dopamine in your brain, which triggers you to repeat the action again. These Budget Parties are to be set up a certain way to stimulate the most pleasure and least pain.

1. Write down a list of everything you and your spouse want for the upcoming month.
    a. Clothes/Shoes
    b. Video Games
    c. Date Night
    d. Activities
    e. Events
2. Produce a solid number for each of these things and a date.
3. Take a break and imagine the fun or enjoyment you will get out of your Want List.

4.   Now list all the recurring bills in a section labeled bills.
  a. Mortgage/Rent
  b. Electric
  c. Water
  d. Gas
  e. Food (Groceries, not restaurants)
  f. Insurance
  g. Maintenance
  h. Other Misc.
  i. Cell Phone
  j. Internet
5.   Remove anything in your bills list that is extra
  a. Subscriptions
  b. TV Cable
  c. Credit Card Payments
  d. Loan Payments
  e. Car Payments
  f. Gym memberships
  g. Other Nonessential Misc.
6.   List these extra bills in another section called "Liabilities".
7.   Debts of all kinds should be listed from highest to lowest, and if you can pay it off in 2 years, do it, if not, develop a plan to systematically sell things and earn extra income to pay it off in 2 years.
8.   Save an agreed-upon amount each paycheck.
  a. 10%

b. $20/Income plus $20/$100 made and $20/Frivolous Expense plus $20/$100 expense

c. $100/Check draft

d. Fifteen percent of employee investing

9. Whatever the method, Save/Invest First, Bills Second, and Wants last. (That does not mean that wants are just what is left or that you get all your wants after the last check; no, it just means your priorities start with what is important first. This could all happen on the same day)

10. Having an "End of Month Balance Sheet" also helps the Budget Parties. They set a precedent for the upcoming month. A target to beat, if you will. It also helps you feel better about your savings and growth. Make this a bottle-popping experience, even if it is low. Do not include any debts in this either; this is strictly positive account balances.

a. Personal Checking - $150

b. Personal Saving - $500

c. 401(k) - $1,000

d. Online Investing App - $250

e. Business Checking - $1,200

f. Cash - $100

g. Total - $3,200

> Even if you cannot spend the money in your retirement account, it is just nice to know it is there. The reason you do not include debts or negatives is because it kills your momentum. You want to look at

and see that you are growing. This is so relieving and empowering at the same time.

- Monthly Budget
  - Relationship spending
    - Dates ($100)
    - Tithes/Offering ($250)
  - Vocational spending
    - Travel ($200) Recurring
    - Licensing/Certification ($500) One-time
    - Relevant Books ($20)
  - Educational spending
    - Classes ($350) Monthly Payment
    - Books/Supplies ($500) One-time
    - Travel ($50)
  - Health/wellness spending
    - Gym membership ($30)
    - Vitamins ($20)
    - Healthy food ($300)
  - Financial spending
    - Investments ($375)
    - Saving for down payment ($250)
    - Buy an asset ($50) - i.e., website, app, domain names, patent, etc.
  - Fun spending
    - Vacation fund ($100)

This is a copy of my own Budget Meeting Dinner Date:

Budget Meeting Dinner Date

Topics:

1. Casting a vision
2. Total bills
3. Debt payoff
4. Total income
5. What we want
6. Discretionary expenses
7. Emergency fund
8. Total assets and growth
9. Our love for one another
10. Embracing our motto (Happy, Healthy, & Holy)

Organization:

1. The vision: we are here apart, together fervently in love just as the seed we planted and watered has sprouted into all that we are today and will be in the future, so to have the roots of our devotion to one another and God has grown. I appreciate this time together that we have set aside to continually grow together in love, devotion, wellness, and dedication to our finances and development on a new level. Can you see that tomorrow's problems will be solved today, and the path will be much smoother forward from here, my love? Here we go.

2. Total bills: $1,002.48; this is an approximate amount of our total drafts for the month of October

3.   Debt payoff: $81,052.52 Mortgage and $66,420.86 Student Loans. I have great news our home will be paid off on April 31st, 2023, and Student Loans will be paid off on June 31st, 2024!

4.   Current Balance: $1,697.87 Expected Income to come: $864.54 Expected Expenses Left to Draft: $764.41 Anticipated Remainder before discretionary expenses: $1798.00

5.   Total income: $5,893.48; this will be a great financial month for us; we also have priorities we can satisfy.

6.   Discussion: home repairs, clothes, dates, impromptu visits, eating out, etc.

Jonathan	Jasmine
Books: $100	Hair & Nails: $300
Drone: $25	Misc.: $100
Car Mount: $25	S

6.   Discretionary Expenses: Gas, Groceries, Home Maintenance

Gas: $150

Groceries: $150

Home Maintenance – Ducts and Septic: $450

7.   Goal is 6 months' income, which is approximately $6014.88 by mid-2021

8.   End the month balance was $31,581.83

9.   Dialogue about how much we love each other, including three things we appreciate about each other, and our futures together

10. Embracing our model, which is Happy, Healthy and Holy.

Resources and References:

1. Budget 2020 Excel spreadsheet
2. Household Budget 2021
2. EOM balances Excel spreadsheet

Daily Schedules are quick and simple breakdowns of the day, allowing you to set aside and proactively plan. Don't get too caught up on any one thing unless it is a time-sensitive item. Beware of over-specifying the obvious and bogging down your schedule with meaningless information about a task. Waking up, putting on clothes, driving to work, taking a shower, and the like are insignificant items that should be left off your schedule. Focus on meaningful actions that lead you closer to your main goal rather than arbitrary information. Especially since you are the only person that is likely going to see your schedule, make it meaningful to you. A precise language that sparks your memory and keeps you focused on the task at hand. Also, know that a daily schedule is not your only template to use, as I stated before. A weekly planner may work better if you have a busy schedule, but for the purposes of the book, a daily schedule is a key to reaching your goals.

- Daily Schedule
  - Relationship
    - Pray for 30mins every day first thing in the morning.

- Smile three times per day in public (be friendly/available)
- Write two things you want in a significant other
  - Vocational
- Call ten new businesses you are interested in Monday-Friday
- Read ten pages of a book pertaining to a business or occupation of interest
- Think of one new thing you can do to improve your current job and do it
  - Educational
- Spend at least 30 to 45 minutes researching the latest information on topics of interest every day
- Study 1 to 2 hours for the course that you are currently in or license your studying
- Write a paragraph about something that you have learned every day (Life Blueprint)
  - Health/Wellness
- Morning Workout everyday 10-15 minutes
- Make a protein-rich breakfast every morning with cinnamon and/or ginger
- Take daily vitamins
- Go to the gym 3-4 times per week to workout key areas of your body
- Run for at least 10 minutes per day
  - Financial
- Make a budget once per month

- ■ Give yourself an allowance and spend it every week
- ■ Track net worth at the end of each month
- ■ Buy assets that generate income (i.e., websites, products, apps, etc.), insignificant things under $100 every week
- ○ Fun
  - ■ Plan your next vacation to the minor detail
  - ■ Visualize this daily
  - ■ Relax every day for 30 minutes uninterrupted
  - ■ Do one thing you like to do for at least 10 minutes daily

Everything must be broken down into smaller units. The smaller you go, the more successful you become. Broad strokes do not achieve success; the path to success is quite narrow and rot with failure. Failure and rejection are the pathways to success. They are used to recalibrate and refocus you towards your ultimate goals. Most people play the game of life to not lose rather than to win. People would rather guarantee a loss on financing a house, a car, or the stuff they buy with a credit card rather than to risk even a penny with an infinite possibility of growth because of the small chance they might lose. If you are currently looking at your portfolio, it is -3.5% on your house, -7.1% on your car, and a $3,000 balance on a -26.99% APY on your credit card. Though fear of loss has crippled you from investing, it does not prevent you from losing. When you get your paycheck, commission, or bonus check, remember these percentages added together is a total of -37.59%, which means every $1 you work for is only worth about .62¢. So, if your paycheck is $3,000 or $1,873.20, you have lost $1,126.80 before you pay the first bill. This is how you should look at every dollar you earn and spend. If you spend money on a liability, it comes with negative effects on your earnings, whereas if you spend it on assets, they come with positive effects on your earnings. In this same example, if instead of your money going into credit cards, mortgage on your home, and car loan, you spent it on a bond that earned 3.5%, mutual funds that earn 7.1%, and a rental property that both appreciate it at 8% per year and provided earnings of $500 per month your paycheck would be worth $4,058. This is a combined interest of +35.27% as opposed to -37.59% which is a substantial difference! This truly can be accomplished with the exact same money you spend on those luxuries that you purchased in the first example. If you pay a mortgage of $900 per month, have a car payment of $300 per month, and swipe your credit card and an average of $500 per month, you will have spent $1,700 and must pay the interest on that as well of $64.05 per month. Whereas if you spend $900 on a rental property mortgage and charge rent of $1,600, after expenses, you will make $500 per month, spend $300 on mutual funds per month at 7.1% interest, and $500 on a savings bond at 3.5% you would earn $1,300 plus 78.80 in interest. This is an example of the same money having vastly different results in your life and this is only just the beginning.

Schematics
Recap, Putting it all Together, and Good Financial Habits

The best processes are those that are repeatable. The most successful businesses in the world are ones that have been able to duplicate themselves. Take for example, McDonald's; this is a simple fast-food franchise, right? Wrong, this is the largest owner of real estate in the world. Making hamburgers and fries certainly can be easily controllable, but without the real estate aspect of the business with title restrictions that mandate the business model as to what you can and cannot do at each location, this business would fail. This is important and is the reason this book is written instructively first and planned second. It is better to start making good habits before you fully understand because results begat belief. Once you see the positive results of your actions, you are inclined to repeat those actions and learn to enhance them. When you join the military, the drill sergeant yells at you to get up early in the morning, workout, run and push your mental and physical capabilities to their limits. Though this is difficult and painstakingly tedious, this process is necessary for making the best soldiers every time. Obedience before knowledge makes for the best outcomes. This is how you create a simple process that is always repeatable.

Understanding what you accomplished mindlessly allows you to make better decisions future as a compounding effect of what you were already doing. This book's titled financial competence because making good decisions and knowing why you made those decisions are two different things. Growing up, my father was a fierce saver, and my mother was a go-getter; she wanted more for her life than living below lowly means. My father was analytical and broke down the ideas my mother had for a business ventures and other income-generating opportunities. They would fight over this profusely, going back and forth. My mother did not have all the facts but wanted to get started anyway. My father wanted all the facts before getting started. These opposing views caused a familial filibuster of sorts, and my father just kept saving, and my mother kept thinking of new things to do without including my father. Eventually, the relationship dissolved, and my father continued to save and made very safe calculated risks with his job's retirement plan and he also purchased a small rental property. My mother started a small business and became a real estate agent. In the end, objectively, my father is better prepared for retirement, and my mother, though not fully prepared for retirement, has a fuller life. Their ideas are not diametrically opposed, and this could have worked had they used my father's analytical skills and saving proclivity and my mother's business acumen and management skills together. Put simply, my father would manage the money, and my mother would manage the people.

This is a perfect example of analysis paralysis that eventually led to their relationship breakdown. I have both in me, and it is the harmony of the two ideas that make for the greatest success. Not being afraid to take the leap of faith while still analyzing and always saving to lock in the growth. This book is based on these two ideas.

The Financial Competent Outline
Foundational Steps

1. Saving – Save 10% of your income in a High-Interest Savings Account or Money Marketing Account. (If you find a dime, save a penny)

    a. Ensure this account is at a different financial institution than your checking account.

    b. Credit Unions are the preferred Savings accounts

    c. Once you have reached 6 months' income, open a savings account in the same financial institution as your checking account for short-term savings goals. Save only 1% (Drip) of your income.

2. Retirement – Invest 15% of your income into your retirement account(s). (401(k), Roth 401(k), 403(b), Roth IRA, Traditional IRA, SIMPLE IRA, etc.)

    a. Invest in your employee retirement plan if your employer matches your contribution. (i.e., if 3%, invest 3%) If there is no match, skip this step.

173

b.   Invest up to 15% of your income into an after-tax (Roth) retirement plan. If 15% of your income is greater than the maximum contribution allowable for your Roth IRA, then invest the rest in your employee retirement plan until maxed out.

c.   Invest the difference of your 15% into a Life Insurance Retirement Plan (LIRP) once you've maxed out both your own as well as your employer's retirement account.

3.   Insurance - Insure all assets, property, health, and life at a fraction of the total of your risk. There is no percentage or flat amount that this should be, however the best metric to decide if you need to insure something is:

a.   If the item or property were to be destroyed, would you suffer a financial loss?

b.   Can you afford to replace the item without dipping into your savings?

c.   Can you afford to live without this item?

Structural Steps

4.   Real Estate – Spend no more than 30% of your income on all factors of your primary property. Make sure you have at least a 10% profit on an investment property.

a.   Primary Residents' expenses should be no more than 30%, including:

  i. Rent/Mortgage

  ii. PMI – Private Mortgage Insurance

  iii. HOA – Homeowners Association Fees

  iv. Property Taxes

  v. Homeowners Insurance

  vi. Utilities

  vii. Groceries

  viii. Home Maintenance

 b. Investment Property should yield a 10% return after the following expenses:

  i. Mortgage

  ii. PMI – Private Mortgage Insurance

  iii. HOA – Homeowners Association Fees

  iv. Property Taxes

  v. Utilities

  vi. Home Maintenance

  vii. Rental Dwelling Insurance

  viii. Property Management

5. Investment – No more than you feel comfortable living without:

 a. Percentage method 5% - 25% per month investing in stocks, bonds, mutual funds, securities, equities, peer-to-peer lending, or other investments.

    b.   Flat Dollar amount is a $10 – $500 investment made monthly in stocks, bonds, mutual funds, securities, equities, peer-to-peer lending, or other investments.

    c.   Either method works great if contributions are consistent and built over time, as in 10% increased to 25% in ten years. This is known as <u>Dollar-Cost Averaging</u> or time in the market rather than timing the market.

6.   Everything Else – Financial Plan the rest of your income wisely on the following items

    a.   Bills (Required and Choice)

    b.   Vacations

    c.   Fun / Dates

    d.   Personal Care (Hair & nails, massages, facials, clothes, eating out, etc.)

    e.   Friends / Family (yes, you should have an aggregate budget for them)

    f.   Books / Education (Always invest in yourself and knowledge)

This is just a brief synopsis of this book in its entirety to make sure you have a full understanding of the steps and make better decisions now. It is never too late to learn and get started. This book is not to go into too deep in detail about any one subject but just to build competence in the subject of finances. I look forward to drafting the next book that will dive into detail about each of these sections to build your Financial Ability.

Gathering Materials
Giving & Tithes

This chapter will be a hard read for those who are money conscious, analytical, or ultra-frugal. Giving? Why would I give and not know how I will get it back? Or why give to someone, an organization, or a church and not know what they are going to do with the money I give them? Being all three, money conscious, analytical, and ultra-frugal, I wondered the same thing not so long ago. I had sat in the same church for years by this point, and every time the dreaded sermon was preached about finances, which really meant tithing, my ears turned off, and I clenched my fist. "There is absolutely no financial incentive or reason to give," I thought. I went out of my way to leave early or miss church altogether on these Sundays. I would volunteer at this church, teach, and stay late to clean up after service, but my money was my own. The pastor of this church dressed very well, drove an expensive car, lived in a mansion, and did not work throughout the week. "This man does not need my money," I thought, and I hated the very mention of giving to him or the church. I drove a nearly 20-year-old car at the time that my wife and I shared, I had not gone shopping for clothes in almost 10 years, only getting new clothes for Christmas and birthday gifts, I was only making $20,000 /year taking care of both my wife and I on that salary, and we lived with a family member, paying them to rent a room. Why would I give someone like that my hard-earned money? I continued this way until I heard it put a way I just couldn't get around.

When you are ready to build a home, you go to the store to buy wood for the frame, studs, and overall structure. Where does the wood come from? A forest filled with trees. These trees are grounded up and chopped into blocks and sheets of wood for you to build. Where do the trees come from? A seed. This minuscule, fragile seed is where these grave and mighty trees come from. It takes approximately 44 trees to build a home of 2,600 square feet which means your home is built not of 44 trees but of 44 tiny seeds that you can hold in your hand. You will not have a home if these small seeds are not planted. The moral of the story is this, you can run from it if you like, but if you do not plant seeds, there are no trees to gather. In America, it is easy to forget that food does not grow in grocery stores, wood is not just found in hardware stores, and water does not just miraculously come out of your faucet. All things must be planted, watered, and harvested. This means hundreds of jobs around the world are designed for the sole purpose of giving you the conveniences you enjoy today. Giving is you planting the seed that will bring much fruit tomorrow for you to harvest. The best builders of homes plant tree farms because they know if they do not plant seeds, no trees will be in supply for the homes they need to build.

All the riches people in the world are prolific givers. Makes you wonder, did they get rich then start giving, or did they give (plant seeds for the structure) all along the way? "If you sow sparingly, you will reap sparingly also, but if you sow generously, you will reap generously as well." This book is about financial competence and giving is a huge component of this fundamental competence. If you are a member of a local church and support the message being preached, sow your seed and tithe a minimum of 10% of your income. This may be the most important message in this entire book for my fellow believers. Plant seeds along the way as you build your finances and make great choices.

Steve Harvey put giving this way on the Steve Harvey Morning Show, "Giving is the key to success… when you give to someone, don't think about it, just give. If you must think about it or if you are in a situation where you give to someone but expect them to do something with the money you gave them, that is not giving; that is a trade. God does not bless trading; He blesses cheerful givers." * We often, like me, withhold giving because we expect the receiver will not do what they are supposed to do with your gift. From here on, do not think of what the person or organization you give to is going to do with the money you give them. Just give and let your sown seed reap a great harvest.

Mustard Seed Actual Size →

to

Mustard Tree

References

1. This Photo by Unknown Author is licensed under CC BY-SA-NC

2. Austen, J. (1973). *Sense and sensibility*. J.M. Dent.

3. Dave Ramsey from The Ramsey Show

4. Olson, J. (2013). *The Slight Edge* (Anniversary ed.). Success Books.

5. https://money.cnn.com/interactive/economy/my-american-success-story-daymond-john/index.html

6. "Spider-Man." Columbia TriStar Home Entertainment, 2002.

7. Skot, S. (2021). *Summary and Analysis of SECRETS OF THE MILLIONAIRE MIND By T. Harv Eker:*

Mastering The Inner Game Of Wealth. Independently published.

8. Ramsey, D. (2018). *The Total Money Makeover Workbook: Classic Edition*. Thomas Nelson Incorporated.

9. Selk, J., Bartow, T., & Rudy, M. (2016). *Organize Tomorrow Today: 8 Ways to Retrain Your Mind to Optimize Performance at Work and in Life* (Reprint ed.). Da Capo Lifelong Books.

10. Covey, S., Foreword, C. J.-, Covey, S. R., & Audio, S. S. (2020). *The 7 Habits of Highly Effective People: 30th Anniversary Edition*. Simon & Schuster Audio.

11. Selk, J., Bartow, T., & Rudy, M. (2016). *Organize Tomorrow Today: 8 Ways to Retrain Your Mind to Optimize Performance at Work and in Life* (Reprint ed.). Da Capo Lifelong Books.

12. Bet-David, Patrick. *Your Next Five Moves: Master the Art of Business Strategy*. Gallery Books, 2021.

13. Ant, Saint Exupery. ANTOINE DE SAINT EXUPERY THE LITTLE PRINCE (DELUXE EDITION) /ANGLAIS (MACMILLAN COLLE). INTERART, 2020.

14. https://www.wanderlustworker.com/the-harvard-mba-business-school-study-on-goal-setting/

15. Harvey, Steve from *The Steve Harvey Morning Show (2022)*

About the Architect (Author)

Jonathan Young was born in the United States in a small suburb east of Atlanta, GA, called Lithonia, GA. In his earlier years in life, he ran track & field at a high-level, placing 4th in the Country in the USATF Championship in 2008. His parent separated and later divorced the same year, and he used this to fuel his drive towards his athletic achievement. He did not have a high GPA in high school. He attended a high-performance school called Dekalb Early College Academy. This high school offered an opportunity to do two years of high school and then two years of college at formerly Georgia Perimeter College, now Georgia State University. He later graduated from Georgia State University with an associate degree in science. All his life, he dreamed of becoming an inventor, he loved math and science with high hopes of becoming an engineer to invent something great one day. Throughout high school and college, Jonathan worked at his mom's nut shop, formerly *The Nutty Bavarian,* now *Nuts About Savannah,* which is still in business today. He was a phenomenal salesperson and was offered many sales positions while working there, one of which was a job in insurance sales. This was the first of three insurance job offerings he turned down, including one his own sister begged him to start for life insurance sales. Just 3 short months after declining the final insurance job opportunity, his best friend (cousin) Tony died in a fatal car accident at the age of 18 years old. He had just lost his job and business and was unable to be of any assistance in the burial of his cousin. This changed Jonathan for the rest of his life. He stopped running from the purpose God obviously wanted him to pursue. Jonathan, on the verge of homelessness, decided to marry his then-girlfriend, now wife Jasmine and the two are happily married. He has worked in the insurance field since 2016 following the tragic loss of his cousin & friend. He has since opened his own insurance agency as well since 2020. Jonathan has dedicated his life to educating all his customers about the real risk of day-to-day life, insurance coverage in general, and helping people gain financial competence as unto the Lord.